JUST LIKE MUM USED TO MAKE

ONE-POT PIES & STEWS

Laura Mason

National Trust

First published in the United Kingdom in 2011 under the title *Good Old-fashioned Pies and Stews*.

This edition published in 2014 for WHSmith by
National Trust Books
10 Southcombe Street
London W14 0RA

An imprint of Anova Books Ltd

Text and recipes © Laura Mason 2011, 2014
Copyright © National Trust Books 2011, 2014

ISBN: 9781907892882

Reproduction by Mission Productions Ltd, Hong Kong
Printed by CT Printing, China

Food photography by Tara Fisher
Home economy by Jane Suthering
Styling by Wei Tang

For more information on game contact Game-to-Eat, The Countryside Alliance Foundation's campaign dedicated to increasing the eating and enjoyment of British wild game. Visit www.gametoeat.co.uk for more information.

Contents

Introduction

STEWS AND PIES are comforting dishes. A hearty beef pie or a meat stew with dumplings or mashed potato suits raw days. Just the smell of it cooking lifts the hearts of those who are feeling low, are weary or cold, or those who are just plain hungry. These dishes use inexpensive cuts of meat and are economical of fuel. What's more, they can be prepared and left in a low oven while the cook does something else, or be reheated at a later date. These are quiet and good-tempered dishes.

Both stews and pies are also much more varied than mere chunks of meat and onions in a thick brown gravy. These do belong to traditional British cookery, but in this book I have explored other possibilities: unthickened sauces that are light and fresh; a large piece of meat instead of cubes; pies served cold instead of hot. There are also recipes for fish and vegetable stews and pies (see pages 182–219).

Acquire a casserole of a size that suits your household, find out how best to use it – and good food will never be far away. My mother gave me a small brown stew jar when I left home, and it became one of my most valued possessions, used so much that my housemates used to ask what the magic pot contained that day. Though they didn't know it, the contents were often chosen by trial and error, but generally they tasted good because I had absorbed the basic method for making a stew at home and learnt to build on it.

A History of Pies & Stews

A STEW IS a dish composed with an end result in mind. In the 18th century, the term for them was 'made dishes'. Martha Bradley, author of *The British Housewife* (1756) said 'Of these there are a great Multitude, and a very rich and pleasing variety … each has its own particular Manner'. Fricassée, jug, haricot, civet, ragoût, daube, braise, fricandeau, hot pot, carbonnade, casserole, blanquette – many of our ideas about stews date from the Georgian period of this time, often derived from French cookery.

Fricassées were slices of meat in a liquid thickened by egg yolks beaten with lemon juice or white wine, a sauce still known in Greek cookery as *avgolemono*. Over time, the mixture lost the acid and was instead thickened by cream or a roux, so now the word is associated with a creamy sauce. Haricot, civet and daube also had specific meanings: 'haricot' denoted something cut into pieces; 'civet' derived from a word for onions but eventually became associated with a hare stew thickened with the blood of the animal; and 'daube' referred to a method used for preparing many foods, cooking them in a pot with aromatics and wine or vinegar. Daubes were originally eaten cold with some of their cooking juices, which jellied as they cooled.

Ragoûts, or 'ragoos', as English speakers called them, arrived with French court cookery at the close of the 17th century. Made from extracts of beef, veal, ham or partridge, and tasty little morsels – mushrooms, truffles, artichoke hearts, asparagus spears, sweetbreads, lambstones (testicles), kidneys, cockscombs – they were poured around joints of meat, whole fish or vegetables. Dishes *à la braise* travelled with them. A joint of meat was placed in a large pan lined with sliced bacon, beef and veal and chopped vegetables; wine, gravy and essence of ham (see page 91), more bacon, beef and veal were added, and the lid sealed on with flour-and-water paste. The whole was set over embers, with some in a recess in the lid, and the contents cooked gently, 'airtight, in order that the aromatic flavouring arising from its contents may be imbibed by the meat or poultry'. So wrote Alexis Soyer in *The Modern Housewife* (1851).

Made by accomplished chefs, these dishes must have been delicious, but the less accomplished and extravagant found them troublesome. For decades, English cooks sniped at French chefs over the skill and the expense required. In time, beef extract replaced strong stocks and gravies, and mushroom ketchup or Worcestershire sauce pepped up insipid mixtures, but ragoos and braises contributed to the notion that stews should be dark and rich.

The more exotic curry is first recorded in English in the mid-18th century, and described a dish made of fowls or rabbits cut up and stewed gently with onions, pepper and coriander seed.

Though later cooks added spicy curry powders, this remained the basic pattern until migrants in the latter part of the 20th century brought a wider range of complex Indian dishes with them.

Some names imply a particular cooking dish. The French donated the word 'casserole', which in the 18th century meant a rice border moulded into the shape of a cooking pot, and holding a savoury mixture. By the late 19th century, it indicated meat and vegetable dishes in closed pots cooked slowly in the oven. Both the pot and the contents became known as casseroles, which became the English idea of stews.

The notion of the container links stews to pies. One type of pie was made with a pastry of coarse flour, water and a little fat. The pastry was inedible and was set by baking, which also cooked the contents – meat, poultry or game. This type of pie crossed over with pottery when fine ceramic containers coloured to imitate pastry were made during a period in the late 18th century when there was a shortage of wheat flour.

Other pies had fillings more akin to a stew: Devonshire Squab Pie contained mutton, onions and apples; Shropshire Pie, rabbit and pork; and Cheshire Pork Pie, pork and apples. In *A New System of Domestic Cookery* (1821), Mrs Rundell remarked that 'There are few articles of cookery more generally liked than relishing-pies, if properly made; and they may be made so of a great variety of things.' Eventually, the lower crust vanished, leaving the type of pie that is still part of our culinary landscape, whether home-made or ready-made (pie vendors were firmly established among street-food sellers in the 19th century). The origin of pies with mashed potato coverings is far more elusive, but unlikely to be much earlier that the first half of the 19th century.

Cooking Pies & Stews

Making a basic stew is about harmonising ingredients and developing flavours – allowing tougher cuts of meat to become tender and blending them with a selection of root vegetables into a well-seasoned and pleasing entity.

Choosing a Container

A container is essential: all you have to discover is which works best for you. Most people acquire a casserole that becomes a favourite because it cooks food well, holds the right amount for the family's needs and looks good. For the past 20 years, a round cast-iron Le Creuset casserole, enamelled in classic flame orange, has been my favourite. If nothing else is available, a large, reasonably heavy pan or deep frying pan will hold a stew for simmering over a low flame (alternatively, it can be put in the oven if it is designed for this, but do remember that the handle will get very hot). Lids for any stewing pan or pot should be close-fitting, although it's always possible to improvise with tinfoil.

Casseroles exist in colourful diversity, and it is nice to have one that looks good at the table. One that can be used both on the hob and in the oven is useful. This generally means stainless or enamelled steel, enamelled cast iron or tinned copper. Cast-iron pots are heavy and expensive to buy, but with care they last for decades. They come in cheerful colours and retain heat well. Try not to drop them, especially on stone floors: cast iron is brittle and enamel chips. Their surfaces also need to be treated with care. Soak to remove any food that is burnt on, and avoid harsh abrasives. Cast iron without enamelling can be used, but any acid ingredients will react with the metal. This is not life-threatening, but it does give the sauce a strange colour. Steel, copper, or combinations of both make durable cooking pots. They are easy to care for unless completely made of copper, in which case the tin lining must be maintained (these are the traditional choice in professional kitchens).

Toughened glass and many ceramic casseroles are inexpensive and durable, and come in designs to suit all tastes and styles of decoration, but they normally can't be used on the hob. Here, a frying pan will be needed for operations requiring direct heat (such as sweating or frying and bringing sauces to the boil), and these ingredients must then be added to the casserole when it is ready to go in the oven. This is not necessarily a disadvantage, but it does mean more washing-up. Of traditional ceramics, stoneware is the most hard wearing. Very rustic earthenware pots (the sort sometimes brought back from Mediterranean holidays) look wonderful and can be used, but they may be better as ornaments: they are often not very durable and are easily chipped, with glazes that tend to be porous or which will craze and so eventually become difficult to clean. Such pots belong to cultures where the slow heat of embers on the hearth or a cooling bread oven are not entirely forgotten, and replacements can be easily and cheaply acquired.

Pie dishes are widely available. The deep-filled pies given in the following recipes require round, oblong or oval pie dishes. They should have wide rims to support the edges of the pastry covering (unless using individual pie dishes of the sort used in pubs, which rarely do). Pie dishes are widely available in earthenware, glass or enamelled iron and share the various advantages and disadvantages of these materials. Traditional English pie funnels shaped as blackbirds are a nice traditional touch to support the pastry in the centre and allow steam to escape.

Meat

Many different recipes for stews exist, but there is a general method for English brown stews, varying only according to taste and the contents of the larder. The method applies principally to meat; fish and vegetables need different management, for which see the relevant sections.

Choose a cut of meat that is appropriate (see individual recipes for suggestions) and cut it into suitable pieces. Cubes that are roughly 2.5cm (1in) along each side are usually suggested, but the pieces can be up to twice as big, especially for venison and beef stews. For larger pieces, the cooking time may be a little longer. Steaks and chops can be stewed without further dividing (meat isn't usually cut into strips except for a fricassée). Remove any obvious bits of gristle or large pieces of fat.

Use kitchen paper to pat the meat dry. For many stews, the meat must first be fried, and wet meat doesn't brown as easily. Dredging the meat with flour before frying also helps to absorb moisture and will thicken the sauce as it cooks.

Marinating is often suggested for meat for stews, especially wine-based marinades. This has little effect on the texture of meat, but is an excellent method for flavouring it. Drain the meat well before cooking and reserve the marinade for the sauce, unless otherwise instructed.

Bacon, or its Italian equivalent, pancetta, should be unsmoked. These provide both fat and flavour for stews. Pancetta can be bought in lardons or cubes, or ask for a thick slice from a delicatessen and cut it up at home. It is usually fairly fatty. Choose bacon carefully, looking for a dry cure

with quite a lot of fat. Bacon tends to be ready-cut into rashers, which are fine for cutting into matchsticks. For cubes, though, you will need to acquire a whole piece and cut it yourself.

Frying

Frying is not an essential step in making a stew – some, including Irish Stew, don't call for it at all – but as a general rule it is a good idea. Browning the meat adds depth of flavour, although it does absolutely nothing to retain the juices, whatever the culinary old wives say.

If starting with bacon or pancetta, allow it to cook until most of the fat has been yielded and it is starting to crisp. Remove the pieces with a slotted spoon and keep to one side while frying the other ingredients in the fat. If necessary, add extra fat to the chosen casserole, or a frying pan if the former isn't flameproof, and allow it to get reasonably hot for frying other ingredients.

Vegetables such as chopped onions are usually fried first to help develop flavour. Fairly high heat and frequent stirring speed things along, but don't let the vegetables burn. Timings given for frying vary enormously across recipes but are usually in the range of 'a few minutes'. Such advice is not especially helpful. Over the years I've come to prefer frying vegetables until quite well cooked. Choose between leaving them on a low heat, checking from time to time and turning to make sure they are cooking evenly; or turning up the heat, frying briskly and turning frequently until they begin to develop golden-brown patches. Watch how they are cooking, and aim for a state in which they have lost some water and the natural sugars they contain have begun to caramelise: the pieces will shrink and start to look golden, especially the onions. If they are allowed to go much darker, they will start to burn. Remove them from the pot with a slotted spoon, allowing as much fat as possible to drain. Use this to fry the meat, in batches if necessary, turning so that the pieces are browned on all sides.

Additional fat is often needed. Most people have their own tastes; I tend to prefer butter. Beef dripping and lard are traditional choices for meaty stews; goose and duck fat are fashionable; olive oil and other vegetable fats are considered healthier. Lamb and mutton fat are best avoided, as they are strongly flavoured and cling to the palate. The recipes suggest what I consider to be minimum amounts, and more may make for easier cooking. Excess fat can always be removed from the surface of a stew at the end.

Vegetables and Seasonings

The base of fried vegetables depends to some extent on the nature of the stew. Onions are routinely used for an English stew. Garlic, celery, carrot or turnip are sometimes added (but avoid leeks, which develop an unpleasant taste and texture when fried). These should be chopped evenly and fairly finely, unless otherwise directed. Ordinary cultivated mushrooms are another frequent addition. Button ones are often left whole, but I prefer to slice any mushrooms and fry until the slices are starting to turn golden. They will soak up whatever fat is in the pan initially; as they cook, the liquid they contain starts to evaporate and they give some of the fat back again.

Seasoning is a matter for individual taste. Salt is the most basic addition; be a little on the mean side when adding it at the start of cooking, and remember that stock cubes and some flavourings such as soy sauce are salty. Always taste a finished stew before adding any more. Once the salt has been added, it is almost impossible to remove. A method sometimes quoted for rescuing a stew that has been over-salted is to peel several large potatoes and put them into the stew to cook. Remove them when done, and they will have absorbed some of the salt. Provided the amount of salt is not vastly overdone, this can be quite effective, but it is better not to add too much salt in the first place.

Pepper is next on the list, almost as ubiquitous as salt for seasoning savoury dishes. Use freshly ground black pepper. Again, amounts are difficult to specify: add and taste until the dish is right for you. Some people like to use combinations of peppercorns – black for aroma, white for heat, green for a mild piquancy, allspice for a slightly perfumed note. Allspice – or Jamaica pepper, as 18th-century cooks called it – is unrelated to pepper but makes a good seasoning for red meats.

Of other spices, a pinch of cayenne or chilli powder wakes up the palate and is especially good in dishes with turkey, wild duck and hare. Nutmeg and mace are both good in meat dishes, as 18th-century cooks knew when assembling meaty ragoos and braised dishes. Buy nutmeg whole and grate, or pound the long yellow-orange blades of mace with a pestle and mortar as needed.

Parsley is a herb that finds its way into many dishes, as a seasoning and a garnish. Chop finely and add just after the liquid when cooking, or scatter over a finished stew for fresh colour and added flavour. Thyme and marjoram are good in many stews, and lemon thyme is delicious in veal and fish dishes – strip the leaves off the stems before using. Tarragon is a herb that people love or hate, but I find it's good with chicken and rabbit. Rosemary can be very strong; use it sparingly.

Recipes often call for a bouquet garni, the little bunch of herbs dropped into a stew after the liquid is added and removed just before the end of cooking. These generally include parsley, a bay leaf, some thyme and other herbs according to the recipe, perhaps with a piece of lemon or orange zest, tied up with thin string or thread. Or use the green leaf of a leek, well washed, to enclose something a little more elaborate: lay a piece of leaf flat, put the herbs and some black peppercorns plus any other desired spices on it, fold the leaf to enclose them and tie up like a parcel. Retrieve and discard a bouquet garni from the sauce before serving a stew.

Some herbs have to be grown – notably chervil, which is difficult to buy; and summer or winter savory, which are both highly aromatic and a little like thyme, but which seem difficult to obtain as cut herbs. Dried herbs are useful, though some dry better than others. Bay, rosemary, thyme and marjoram lose least in terms of perfume. One teaspoon of dried herb is equivalent to about 1 tablespoon of the same freshly chopped, so when adding to dishes treat with respect.

Mushroom products of various descriptions are also useful for seasoning, following the habits of 250 years ago (if the recipes are to be believed, those who could afford it were consuming enormous quantities of truffles and morels). Field mushrooms were made into strongly flavoured ketchup, a version of which is still available – try adding a little to a beef or game stew. Soak dried porcini mushrooms to add savour to meat stews or make a good vegetarian stock. Italian delicatessens sell various truffle and porcini pastes in jars. They are quite expensive, but are a good way of adding such flavours to stews.

Adding Liquids
Water is the most basic cooking medium of all, which can be used in default of any other cooking liquids.

A well-made stock adds depth of flavour and even a simple one made by simmering a carrot and onion with the bones from a Sunday chicken or a rib of beef will help a stew along. If time and resources allow, make a more complex one using bones from meat appropriate to the recipe; the stew will be so much the better. Strong, well-reduced beef stock was essential in the French-influenced cookery of England in the 18th and early 19th centuries, and was added to all kinds of dishes, probably giving them all a similar flavour. Stock cubes tend to share this disadvantage, but are good enough if nothing else is available. Commercially produced stocks have become available in other forms – in plastic pouches, jars or as heavily reduced pastes – and are good alternatives to home-made ones.

Wine is frequently used in stews and casseroles. The usual basic rule applies: if you wouldn't drink it, don't cook with it. This doesn't mean choosing a fine vintage wine, but do use a good wine, and not the end of a bottle that has lingered in a warm kitchen until it has turned to vinegar. It should always be added at an early stage of cooking for the flavour to mellow. Wine makes a good marinade – for instance, in a recipe based on *boeuf à la bourguignonne* (see page 169). Fortified wines, especially port, are often used with game.

Beer, likewise, is a good addition to many stews, especially those made with beef or game such as hare or venison. Like wine, it can be used as a marinade and needs to be cooked for a long time to get the best out of the flavour. Recent fashions in brewing have tended towards strongly hopped brews – these should be avoided for cooking because they make stews cooked with them unpalatably bitter. Look for traditionally English mild, bitter or brown ale; winter ales, with a higher alcohol content and slight sweetness, can also be good.

Cider is another traditional product that is sometimes added to stews. Use a well-made variety and allow it long cooking to mellow the flavour. It is often chosen as a cooking liquid for rabbit, pork and, to a lesser extent, chicken.

Juices and other fruit-based products also have a role to play. Apple juice provides a sweeter, less assertive alternative to cider; add some lemon juice if it tastes too sweet. Another possibility is verjuice, the juice of unripe grapes or apples. Formerly, this must have been prepared in every large kitchen in the country, but it went out of use sometime around the end of the 17th century. It has been revived by a few winemakers and can be bought bottled and pasteurised from good delicatessens. Less aggressive in flavour than vinegar and more complex than lemon juice, it adds a gentle fruity acidity to sauces.

Lemon juice can be used to add a slightly acid note to any recipe requiring it. Orange juice has a more dominant flavour, but lifts stews made with red meat, and I find it a good flavouring for liver. Redcurrant jelly is a traditional way of adding a sweet–sour fruitiness to game stews in British game cookery, but many other fruit jellies are available – try quince, plum or damson.

In the past, recipes calling for vinegar had the British cook reaching for a bottle of dark brown malt vinegar (originally a by-product of brewing beer). These days, it is considered to have an aggressive flavour, although it was often used in dishes of braised steak, and a little can be added towards the end of cooking in beer-based stews. Wine or cider vinegars add acidity without the underlying maltiness, but in recent years balsamic vinegar has swept all before it. Traditionally made aged balsamic vinegar from Modena in northern Italy is expensive and far too precious to be added to stews, but cheaper versions add a sour–sweet, caramel flavour and are good in updated versions of Stewed Steak (see page 58).

Thickening

A common method for thickening stews is essentially based on the idea of a roux. For beef stews, flour is added at the start, often used to toss the meat, or shaken into the fat left over from frying. Liquid is added to make the sauce and the mixture cooks down to thicken the gravy. This is a method best used with stews cooked in the oven, because it has a tendency to stick to the base of the pan when used on direct heat – either add enough liquid to make the sauce quite thin at the start, or keep stirring and top up if necessary.

Stews cooked without added flour are often thickened at the end. *Beurre mani*é is one option; this indicates equal quantities of butter and flour worked together to a paste. When cooking is complete, uncover the stew and dot the mixture over the surface in small pieces. Shake the pan to absorb it, or stir gently. The butter should melt into the mixture, distributing the flour to thicken it. Once again, do not allow the dish to boil again or reheat it. About 30g (1oz) of flour and 30g (1oz) of butter is ample for a stew for four (see Ragoût of Oxtail, page 60).

Adding arrowroot or cornflour is a simple way of thickening sauces; arrowroot produces a finer result. Put the arrowroot or cornflour in a cup or small bowl and add a little cold water, mixing to obtain a smooth thin paste. Pour this into the hot (not boiling) stew and stir to distribute evenly. Heat gently to bring the mixture to the boil and thicken it. It should take only a couple of minutes to do this. The flavour is neutral and there are no problems about reheating dishes thickened this way, although prolonged heat may affect the starch and thin the sauce a little.

For stews based on pale meats, fish or vegetables, an egg yolk mixture can be used, as in a fricassée. Beat the yolks together with the lemon juice, wine, vinegar or cream. Remove the dish from the heat and allow it to cool a little, then stir in the mixture. It should thicken the sauce lightly – you may also need to reheat it carefully to encourage this, but avoid too much heat, or the egg will cook and curdle the sauce. Don't allow it to boil again. Three egg yolks and about 100ml (3½fl oz) of the liquid ingredient will thicken a stew for four people. This method has a significant effect on flavour (and colour if cream is added), and should not be used with stews intended for reheating.

Some ingredients for stews act naturally as thickeners. Potatoes often start to break down in the sauce and some people positively encourage this, stirring to help it along, because they like the texture. Very well-made stocks, especially veal-based ones, are gelatinous and gain body as the liquid evaporates. In the past, their flavour, texture and transparency were valued for adding to rich stews of all descriptions; cooks made and kept supplies of well-reduced veal stock, which they called glaze. This does require making stock yourself, but if you discover a meat stew is on the liquid side at the end of cooking, try ladling some of the broth into a separate pan and boiling hard to reduce it. This concentrates the flavour (so don't season until the end) and also adds a little more body to the stock.

A little butter added right at the end of cooking also adds flavour and gloss – but don't reheat, or it will separate out.

Times and Temperatures

One of the best things about stews is their flexibility. Combine the ingredients, pour into a casserole, cover and put in a low oven. If the pot seems to need an extra seal, put a layer of tinfoil or a double sheet of greaseproof paper, trimmed to fit, under the lid. Leave well alone for 2–3 hours. At the end of this time, the result should be a perfectly good stew; put it back for a bit longer if it's not quite done. The gentle heat of the bottom oven of an Aga is ideal. If you are not cooking to a deadline and can review progress occasionally, that is really all you need to do.

However, I have suggested times and temperatures in the recipes. A slow oven means anything from as low as the oven allows through 140–150°C (275–300°F, Gas mark 1–2). Times will be a little more or a little less depending on how accurate the thermostat is. The tougher the meat, the longer and slower cooking should be. Higher temperatures – say a moderate oven of 180°C (350°F, Gas mark 4) – are fine with meat that is already fairly tender, such as poultry or young game birds. Cooking times are quicker, say between 1 hour and 1½ hours, for chicken portions. Pies need a different approach, as the pastry needs to set – and to rise, if using puff pastry (see page 34).

Cooking stews on the hob is probably less easy for us than it was in the past. To do this well, the liquid needs to be kept just below boiling – only the slightest movement should be apparent on the surface. The simmering plate of an Aga does very well, but neither gas nor electricity seem capable of the really low heat needed. Nor have I ever had much success with the various mats sold to put under pans to distribute low heat evenly across the base – but if they work for you, then that is an option. Slow cookers can also be used for cooking stews, and need even less attention. Follow the manufacturer's instructions for heating them up and in relation to settings for different types of meat.

Removing Fat

A cooked meat stew often has a fair amount of excess fat on the surface, either from frying the ingredients in the initial stages or from fat that is given up by the meat during cooking. If serving the stew immediately, remove as much fat as possible by skimming it off with a spoon or blotting the surface with kitchen paper, trying not to pick up any of the sauce in the process. Otherwise, allow the stew to cool and then chill in the fridge overnight. The next day, it is easy to lift the solidified fat off the surface.

Reheating

With the exception of stews made from veal or game birds (in which the meat tends to dryness), most meat stews taste better after reheating the next day, when the flavours have had a chance to mellow and blend. This offers the convenience of being able to make a complex dish the day before it is needed – or the week or month before if stored in the freezer. Store cooled stews in a cold larder or the fridge overnight, or pour into a suitable container for freezing. Leave any final thickenings or additions such as breadcrumbs or dumplings until you are ready to reheat a stew. Those based on vegetables or fish don't reheat well, as the fresh flavours and subtle textures are lost in the process.

A frozen stew is best defrosted for several hours before needed. Don't worry too much if the sauce appears to separate; it should come back together with a little stirring when the mixture is hot again.

For reheating, put the mixture into a suitable serving dish. Heat in a moderate oven (180°C, 350°F, Gas mark 4) for about 30 minutes or until the mixture is, in that old-fashioned English phrase, 'piping hot' – in other words, not far off boiling; stir from time to time. If you prefer, reheat the stew gently in a pan, but watch carefully and stir frequently to make sure the mixture heats evenly and doesn't stick to the pan. A little water can be added to thin particularly thick sauces during the process if desired. Add any finishing touches such as dumplings or bread-based toppings as the stew is reheated.

US Conversion Chart

Dry measures

1 US cup	50g (2oz)	breadcrumbs
1 US cup	75g (3½oz)	rolled oats
1 US cup	120g (4oz)	white flour
1 US cup	150g (5½oz)	wholemeal flour
1 US cup	175g (6oz)	raisins, sultanas, prunes
1 US cup	200g (7oz)	rice, pearl barley
1 US cup	225g (½lb)	cream cheese

Liquid measures

¼ US cup	50ml (2fl oz)	
1 US cup	250ml (8fl oz)	
2 US cups (1 US pint)	475ml (16fl oz)	

Butter and lard measures

¼ stick	25g (2 tbsp)	
1 stick (1 US cup)	100g (8 tbsp)	

Unless otherwise stated, salted butter, plain white flour, ordinary table salt and granulated sugar can be used for the recipes in this book. Try to use unwaxed oranges or lemons where zest or peel is required.

Accompaniments for Pies & Stews

ACCOMPANIMENTS DIVIDE roughly into two — garnishes that provide contrasts in texture or enhance the flavour of the stew, or items that complement it, mopping up the gravy and adding bulk.

Bread was originally used to mop up sauces and gravies, and is still a good idea to serve with many stews; some fresh crusty bread is particularly good with light chicken, fish or vegetable stews. Cooks in previous centuries used sliced bread, toasted or fried as sippets and croûtons (see page 29) to give contrasts in texture to softer dishes.

In the 17th and 18th centuries, pudding (of the plain suet variety) might have provided an alternative to bread. The idea is still with us in the form of suet dumplings dropped in the stew towards the end of cooking. Make them plain, or add seasonings (see page 24) — filling food to go with hearty meat stews. For lighter stews make tiny delicate breadcrumb dumplings of a type my mother called butterballs (see page 26) — these are more a garnish than filler.

Potatoes became a ubiquitous accompaniment for stews in the late 19th century. Use whichever variety you prefer, and prepare them however you want – but perhaps the best, and certainly the most comforting, is mashed potatoes. One tablespoon of mild mustard or a tablespoon of creamed horseradish (or more to taste) are good additions to mashed potatoes served with beef stews.

For game stews, try a purée of potatoes and celeriac mashed together: use two large celeriac, peeled and cut into chunks, and about 700g (1½lb) potatoes, also peeled and cut in chunks. Cook in separate pans, remembering that the celeriac will take almost twice as long as the potatoes to cook. Drain both throughly and mash together or put through a vegetable mill. Beat in about 30g (1oz) butter, seasoning as required and 100ml (3½fl oz) warm milk (or milk and cream mixed if feeling self-indulgent). Alternatively, mash in parsnips instead of celeriac (particularly good with beef dishes such as Stewed Steak, see page 58), or turnip, also good with beef, or add a few peeled garlic cloves to the cooking water and mash them with the potatoes. Parsnips or celeriac mashed on their own also make good accompaniments. Or, try making a pan of Stovies (see page 211).

Other things to eat with stews include plain boiled rice for spiced or creamy dishes, or pasta such as papardelle with game stews. Both rice and pasta have their place in the traditions of English food, but polenta hasn't. It is, however, one of the best accompaniments to game stews, especially hare (see Hare and Beer Stew, page 174).

Dumplings

Suet dumplings are comforting companions for a meaty stew, particularly one made with beef. They probably share a common ancestor with suet puddings, and are rib-sticking food intended to stretch precious supplies of other, more expensive ingredients. They are simple to make and easy to vary with different flavourings. Make the mixture just before you want to cook it. Plain flour mixed with 1 teaspoon baking powder can be used instead of self-raising flour if desired. The stew they are destined for needs to be completely cooked. Bear in mind that the dumplings will need about 25 minutes to cook after they have been added.

serves
4

120g (4oz) self-raising flour
60g (2¼oz) shredded suet
about 120ml (4fl oz) water, to mix
a pinch of salt

to flavour
1 generous tablespoon chopped parsley
   with a little thyme and marjoram;

or 1 generous teaspoon mustard powder and about 1 tablespoon chopped parsley or chives; or 1 generous tablespoon creamed horseradish; or a little chopped fresh tarragon

If you are reheating a stew, it is best to start this off before adding the dumplings. Put all the dry ingredients into a bowl. Add the flavouring ingredients if desired. Then add about two-thirds of the water and mix. The mixture should be fairly soft but not too sticky. Add a little more water if it seems dry. Form into balls the size of a large walnut and drop them on top of the stew.

If the stew is cooking in the oven, leave it uncovered after adding the dumplings. They will crisp slightly on top, and may colour a little in the heat. If the stew is cooking on the hob, drop the dumplings into the liquid and cover the pan.

Cook for a further 20–30 minutes in the oven on 180°C (350°F, Gas mark 4) until the dumplings are cooked through and slightly golden on top. Alternatively, allow about 20 minutes for a stew cooking on the hob.

TIP: For dumplings to be cooked on top of a stew in the oven, try replacing 40g (1½oz) of the flour with 40g (1½oz) dried breadcrumbs – this makes the surface crisper.

Norfolk Dumplings

Norfolk dumplings are made from ordinary bread dough. Instead of baking in the conventional manner, the dough is cooked in boiling water. They make a good accompaniment to stews with a generous amount of strongly flavoured gravy, such as those based on hare.

serves
6

1 teaspoon dried yeast
150ml (5fl oz) hand-hot water
250g (9oz) flour, plus extra for dusting
1 scant teaspoon salt

Add the yeast to the water and leave in a warm place for a few minutes until frothy. Stir the yeast mixture into the flour and salt and knead well, then allow it to rise for about 1 hour or until doubled in size.

Have ready a large pot of boiling salted water. Divide the dough into six, make into balls and drop into the water. Keep them boiling for about 20–25 minutes. The dumplings will expand a little as they cook. Drain and serve with the stew. Don't try to cut them, but pull apart with two forks.

Forcemeat Balls & Butterballs

Forcemeat balls are considerably more elegant than dumplings. They are a traditional garnish for game dishes such as Jugged Hare (see page 172) and were also added to pie fillings. In the past they were usually fried, but can be cooked in the oven if preferred. Forcemeat balls can also be made very small. It took me years to realise that 'butterballs' – small delicate dumplings my mother served in soups – were essentially forcemeat balls made without flavourings.

serves 4

120g (4oz) fresh breadcrumbs
60g (2¼oz) butter
1 egg yolk
zest of 2 large lemons
3 tablespoons chopped parsley
1 tablespoon chopped thyme leaves
a generous grating of nutmeg
1 teaspoon salt
black pepper
butter, for frying

To make the forcemeat, put all the ingredients into the goblet of a food processor or blender. Process for a few seconds to give a smooth paste. Shape this into walnut-sized balls and fry them gently in butter, turning frequently, for about 10 minutes. Add them to the stew before serving.

Alternatively, put them into a baking dish and bake in the oven for about 20 minutes on 180°C (350°F, Gas mark 4).

For butterballs, use only the breadcrumbs, butter, egg yolk and a pinch of salt. Make them very small – the size of hazelnuts – and poach gently in the stew for 5–10 minutes. Excellent with fish or vegetable stews such as Sarah's Summer Vegetable Stew (see page 209).

Cobbler Topping for Stew

This is a soft dough cut into rounds and placed in a layer over a stew or other sauce. The idea found its way into English recipe books in the 1960s and 1970s as an alternative to dumplings or pastry. The dough is reminiscent of a savoury scone mix – or perhaps one should say a North American biscuit dough, since the idea seems to have come from there. Use instead of dumplings with beef and vegetable stew; on hare cooked with beer, or instead of pastry on venison and mushroom pie. As with dumplings, the stew should be almost cooked or heated through before the topping is added, and cooking needs to be finished off in the oven.

serves
4

150g (5oz) plain flour, plus extra for
    rolling out
2 teaspoons baking powder
pinch salt
30g (1oz) butter
1 egg, beaten
1–2 tablespoons milk

Sift the flour, baking powder and salt together. Rub in the butter. Mix to a soft dough with the egg, adding a little milk if necessary.

Roll out to 2cm (¾in) thick and cut into rounds 5cm (2in) in diameter. Arrange these over the top of the stew – some people try to overlap them so that the edges crisp a little, browning and adding contrasts of texture. Brush the tops with milk.

Turn the oven up to 230°C (450°F, Gas mark 8) and cook for 15–20 minutes, or until the topping is well risen and brown. Keep an eye on it to make sure it doesn't burn.

Using Bread as a Topping

Although bread – fresh or as toasted or dried sippets – was often served with a dish, this wasn't used on top to add texture. Maybe this was because stewing and braising, carried out in a pan with a tightly sealed lid, meant that it was futile to add bread at the start: it would simply disappear into the sauce.

A friend made the Belgian dish *carbonnade à la flamande* (beef cooked in beer) for me, covering the surface with thin slices of baguette, which had been lightly spread with a mixture of mustard and butter and allowed to crisp in the oven. Strangely, in view of the taste for bread-and-butter pudding, the idea has never transferred to savoury dishes in English cookery, but sliced bread, lightly buttered or dipped in oil, makes an excellent topping for stew. To try this, cut half a large baguette or one small one into oblique slices. Soften about 50g (2oz) butter and mix with 1 teaspoon mustard. Spread thinly over the slices. Put these in an overlapping layer on top of a stew and heat in the oven until the bread is turning crisp. Don't let it scorch.

Alternatively, use a more standard English-style white bread: cut the crusts off, then cut the slices into triangles and dip lightly in melted butter or olive oil as for the Butterbean Casserole (see page 218). Place them on top of the stew, overlapping them as if to make bread-and-butter pudding, and allow to crisp and brown lightly in the oven at about 200°C (400°F, Gas mark 6).

Sippets and Croûtons

Sippets in the English tradition, and croûtons derived from French cookery, both provide contrasting textures and make a good garnish for stews, especially if cut into pretty shapes.

Sippets are thin, crisp little pieces of bread used to garnish soft mixtures such as hashes. Try them with fish stews. To make them, use thin slices of ordinary white bread, preferably slightly stale. Cut off the crusts, and cut into triangles or slender oblongs, or make heart shapes using a pastry cutter. Toast, or dry gently in a low oven to crisp the bread, then use to garnish the stew.

Think of croûtons, and we normally picture bread cut into small dice and fried in butter. For garnishing stews, though, they were larger, cut from slices of white bread. They could be triangular, kite-shaped or heart-shaped. Fry gently in butter (you may need a generous amount) and drain on kitchen paper, then serve with hare or venison stews.

Breadcrumbs

We don't use breadcrumbs as much as we could. One of the nicest finishes I know for a fish or vegetable stew is fresh breadcrumbs fried in a little olive oil with flavourings, an idea loosely based on southern European traditions.

2 tablespoons olive oil
50g (2oz) fresh white breadcrumbs
leaves from 3–4 sprigs thyme
1 garlic clove, peeled and crushed
1 teaspoon lemon zest
pinch salt

Heat the olive oil in a frying pan and sauté the breadcrumbs gently until they begin to turn golden brown. Stir in the thyme, garlic and lemon zest and add a pinch of salt. Turn off the heat. Scatter over the surface of the stew just before serving.

Other Final Additions

THE SIMPLEST METHOD for adding more flavour and colour to a stew is to scatter over chopped herbs. Parsley is the most common, its brilliant green quoted as a decoration for almost every savoury dish in the English repertoire. It is absolutely fine, if a little overused. Chervil is pretty, its feathery leaves adding a mild aniseed note and it's good with fish. Green coriander has become nearly as ubiquitous as parsley on spiced dishes of Indian origin. Chives are good on many dishes; or try finely sliced spring onions on recipes involving potatoes, or chopped tarragon on chicken or rabbit stews. Try finely chopped parsley, garlic and lemon zest on lamb or chicken casseroles. For a more exotic note, chopped green coriander with some very finely sliced fresh green chilli and a little garlic can lift all sorts of dishes, especially those with lamb, duck or fish.

Pesto is another good non-traditional addition, especially in stews involving tomatoes, as is a little grated Parmesan or other strong cheese, especially for vegetable stews. Or, for stews that begin by frying dice or matchsticks of bacon, keep some of the cooked bacon to one side and scatter over the top of the stew just before serving.

Shortcrust Pastry

Shortcrust pastry is simple to make. Use lard for a very short pastry or butter for good flavour – or a mixture of the two. Solid vegetable fat and margarine can both be used for pastry making, but reduced fat and low-fat spreads are unsuitable.

serves 4

300g (11oz) flour mixed with a
    generous pinch of salt
150g (5oz) lard, butter, or lard and
    butter mixed
6–8 tablespoons cold water

Put the flour and salt in a bowl. Cut the fat into 1cm (½in) dice and add to the bowl. Using the tips of your fingers, lightly rub the fat into the flour until the mixture resembles fine breadcrumbs. Then add enough water to make a coherent dough – a little less or a little more may be needed, depending on how dry the flour is. Shape it into a ball, wrap in foil and put in a cool place for at least 30 minutes to rest before using.

Puff Pastry

Making *pâte feuilletée* (the true puff pastry of the French kitchen) requires skill and time. This recipe is a simplified version, known in British cookery as 'rough puff pastry'. It won't rise as much as true puff pastry, but is still good. Alternatively, puff pastry is easily available from the chill cabinets of supermarket freezers, either as blocks or ready-rolled sheets. It makes the cook's life much easier. The fat must be cold from the fridge. Use a sharp knife to cut the pastry, and be careful not to crush the cut edges or get egg wash on them, or it won't rise as nicely.

serves
4

250g (9oz) flour, plus extra for
    working and rolling
175g (6oz) chilled fat (equal
    quantities of butter and lard)
iced water
salt

Put the flour in a bowl and add about ½ teaspoon salt. Using the coarse side of a grater, grate the butter and lard into the flour (dipping the fat into the flour periodically helps to make this easier). Once all the fat is in, start adding iced water, a tablespoon at a time, stirring the mixture with your hand until a stiff paste forms. Don't overdo the water: the mixture needs to be coherent but not sticky.

Turn on to a floured worksurface and work for a moment, just enough to make sure the mixture is even. Then roll out into an oblong three times as long as it is wide; turn the top third down towards you and the bottom third up to cover this. Turn 90 degrees clockwise and repeat the rolling and folding process, then chill for 30 minutes. Repeat this rolling and folding process twice more, give the pastry a final rest and it is ready for use. It can be made a day in advance; if you do this, wrap it in foil or clingfilm and store in the fridge overnight.

Covering a Pie

THE METHOD is essentially the same, whether using shortcrust or puff pastry.

Use a traditional English pie or pudding dish with an edge about 1cm (½ in) wide. Put in the filling, and allow it to cool if it is hot. A pie funnel in the centre is a nice traditional touch, especially in large pies. Roll out the pastry on a floured surface to just over 5mm (¼in) thick, aiming for a shape roughly equivalent to the dish, but a little larger. From this, cut a strip about 1.5cm (⅝in) wide, long enough to go around the edge of the dish.

Using a pastry brush dipped in water, wet the edge of the dish all the way round, then stick the pastry strip to it. Trim the rest of the pastry to the size of the top of the dish. Wet the top of the pastry strip, then cover with the rest of the pastry. Press the two layers lightly together with your fingers (shortcrust pastry can be crimped; cut nicks in the edge of puff pastry to scallop the edge). Cut an air vent in the middle or make a hole where the pie funnel is. Gather together any scraps of pastry, re-roll and cut into leaves or other shapes as desired, then wet the reverse and use to decorate the pie.

Brush the top of the pie lightly with beaten egg, or a little cream or milk. Put shortcrust-covered pies into a moderately hot oven at 200°C (400°F, Gas mark 6) for about 20 minutes, then turn the heat down to 180°C (350°F, Gas mark 4) to complete the cooking. Puff pastry needs to rise as well as cook through. Start this in a hot oven at 220°C (425°F, Gas mark 7), turning down to 180°C (350°F, Gas mark 4) for the remainder of cooking time.

The pie dish can be lined with pastry before the filling is added if desired, but gravy makes it soft, and it can be difficult to get the lower crust properly browned in the centre. Using a metal pie dish and putting it on a hot baking sheet before cooking helps.

Beef & Veal

AS A CHILD, stewed steak was a dish I sometimes found waiting for me on returning home from school on a winter's evening. It wasn't until I began researching this book that I realised those homely dishes of well-cooked beef with a few onions and a little gravy have a culinary pedigree dating back to the 17th century, possibly further. Over the centuries, the liquid used has varied from wine, beer, vinegar or stock to just water, and the seasoning from onions, garlic or spices to the many proprietary sauces that became popular in the 19th century. The idea remains the same, though the method has changed; originally, the meat was gently cooked, placed between two dishes and set over a few embers.

Steaks in the past were normally cut from a rump of beef, an alternative to stewing it as a large piece of meat. An insight into how this aided household management was given by Alexis Soyer in 1851. A rump of beef was 'a very excellent and most useful joint to be continually kept in a country-house, where you may be at some distance from a butcher's, as, when hung up in a cool larder, it keeps good for a considerable time, and you never feel at a loss should some friends call unawares; after a third of it has been removed for steaks … the remainder makes an excellent joint, roasted or braised … or stewed.'

Large joints of beef were boiled with herbs and root vegetables in the 17th century. For the elegant dishes introduced around the start of the 18th century, the meat received all the standard treatments given out by cooks and chefs in great houses. The names of the dishes – *à la braise*, *à la daube*, *à la mode*, *à la royale*, in ragoo – give away their French origin. They were rich and savoury with wine, spices, herbs, bacon or ham, beef gravy (stock) and veal cullis (a strong extract), garnishes of mushrooms, morels and truffles, or ragoos of sweetbreads and other luxurious morsels. Except for Beef à la Mode (see page 46), they were largely forgotten again in the 19th century, although their European descendants, such as *boeuf à la bourguignonne*, were periodically rediscovered in France by English cookery writers (see page 169 for a version with venison).

The modest domestic beef stews of the type we know, with onions and root vegetables, had emerged by the 19th century. Diced stewing beef, sold cheaply from market stalls on Saturday evenings as 'pieces', was within the means of even the poverty-stricken housewives of Lambeth in 1910, recorded by Maud Pember-Reeves in *Round about a Pound a Week* (1910).

Beef steaks were also regarded as good fillings for pies, earlier ones being quite elaborate and often involving highly seasoned forcemeat. This element disappeared in the 18th century, although oysters were frequently added until disease and pollution eradicated most of the fisheries in the mid-19th century. The filling of steak and kidney, now thought of as an iconic dish of English cookery, was developing at this period, as were the pastry-covered meat and potato pies of northern industrial areas and the mashed potato-topped cottage pie. As for hearty steak and ale pies, there is little evidence for them before the 1960s, however much breweries might like us to believe otherwise.

Attitudes to veal have become complicated in recent years, but there are numerous recipes for it in books from the past and it was obviously a commonplace meat. Valued for its pale colour and delicate flavour, it was made into fricassées, or cooked with spring vegetables; for something more savoury, it might be served braised or with a ragoo. One particular dish, a fricandeau of veal, appears in many recipe books; the word shares the same French origin as fricassée, and refers to braised slices of veal taken from the leg of the animal. The English tradition also includes many recipes for olives of veal, rolled around stuffing mixtures and cooked alone or made into Veal and Ham Pie (see page 64).

Both beef and veal were essential as foundations for elaborate stews and braises in the 18th century. Beef bones and coarse 'gravy beef' gave flavour and colour to broths and stocks essential to all meat dishes. Veal made pale gelatinous stocks that could be slowly reduced to glazes, covering the finished dish with a transparent glistening coat. Both meats were also added as slices to give savour to braises, and minced for forcemeats, and veal sweetbreads were frequently added to 18th-century ragoos.

Cooking Beef & Veal in Stews & Pies

BEEF FOR STEWING or braising is generally cut from the forequarter of the animal. This provides stewing and braising steak from the neck and shoulder, and shin, which has a characteristic patterning of collagen through the slices. Shin is good for very slow-cooked stews, in which the collagen dissolves and adds body to the sauce. The hindquarter also provides meat suitable for braised dishes, particularly from the top rump – this is relatively tender, good in stewed-steak dishes. Flank, although fatty, is also good for slow cooking. Other cuts of beef for stews are skirt, oxtail and ox cheek, all of which require liquid and a low oven for several hours to make them really tender, but they are inexpensive and well-flavoured. Large pieces of beef can be braised. Brisket may have a complex interleaved structure and a tendency to shrink in cooking, but has good flavour. Topside is a more elegant alternative.

Stewing steak can be bought ready diced, although some people prefer to buy a piece and trim and cut it themselves. It doesn't always have to be cut into small cubes; you may prefer larger pieces, and some stews, such as *à la bourguignonne*, call for it to be cut slightly differently. A standard English-style stew of beef will take 2–3 hours to cook slowly. For a pie filling, cook the meat in its sauce and cool a little before covering with pastry.

Beef shares some characteristics with venison: both are red meats with pronounced flavours that react well to wine and herb sauces and which benefit from slow cooking. Recipes can be used more or less interchangeably.

Veal is quite different – pale, delicate, lean and with a tendency to dryness. It is expensive and sometimes difficult to buy, but can be delicious. Stewing veal can sometimes be purchased ready-diced, or buy breast or neck of veal and trim and cut it up at home. It is good in fricassée-style sauces and was the original meat for the recipe given in a following chapter as Pork Meatballs with Saffron Sauce (see page 103). A creamy sauce, as given for Turkey Fricassée (see page 130), is another possibility. Try not to overcook the meat. Traditional methods of overcoming dryness included larding, cooking the meat with slices of bacon, and adding rich forcemeats (see Veal and Ham Pie, page 64).

In English traditions, mildly acid flavours were used with veal; sorrel was favoured, but you can use lemon juice instead, or even, as in the recipe for Spring Stew of Veal (see page 62), gooseberries. For richer, meatier dishes, dry sherry is an excellent addition to the cooking liquid.

Christmas Beef Stew

The inspiration for this was plum pottage, a beef broth made with dried fruit and spices, and laced with alcohol. A tradition at Christmas in 17th- and 18th-century England, it was made in huge quantities and served as a soup. Exactly what this was like isn't obvious — the word pottage (or porridge, as sometimes used) suggests something quite thick, but it may have been thinner, more like a broth or clear soup with a sweet–sour flavour. This version produces something akin to a tagine. If possible, ask the butcher to slice the beef with the bone in.

serves
6

1.5kg (3lb 4oz) shin of beef, in slices
water, to cover
6 cloves
4cm (1½in) piece cinnamon stick
2 teaspoons ground ginger
30g (1oz) sugar
160g (5¼oz) prunes, without stones

60g (2¼oz) raisins
40g (1½oz) currants
zest of ½ orange
zest of 1 lemon
100–150ml (3½–5fl oz) port
juice of 1 lemon
salt

Put the meat in a casserole and just cover with water. Cover and cook on 140°C (275°F, Gas mark 1) for 2–2½ hours, by which time the meat should be tender. Drain the liquid into a pan. When the meat is cool enough to handle, pick out the lean meat in nice chunks and set aside. Add the debris and any bones to the stock, and simmer again until the liquid is reduced to about half the original volume. Strain, reserving the liquid. Skim off any fat that rises to the surface.

Put the meat, spices, sugar, dried fruit, and orange and lemon zest into a casserole and add the reserved stock. Heat and then simmer gently – or in a low oven, 160°C (325°F, Gas mark 3) – for about 1 hour.

Then add about 1 teaspoon salt, taste, and if it is still on the insipid side, add a little more until the flavour seems about right. Add most of the port and about half the lemon juice. Taste again and adjust with more port, lemon juice or salt as you feel necessary.

Heat gently again until it comes back to the boil and serve. A good accompaniment is a mixture of potatoes and parsnips, mashed together.

Beef à la Mode

Beef à la Mode appeared in cookery books in the first half of the 18th century, along with Beef Royale, Beef à la Daube and other obviously French-derived dishes. The recipe was used for large pieces of meat; 2.25–2.7kg (5–6lb) was typically quoted. It can be served hot or cold. You may want to include a pig's foot when cooking; this will help the juices set to a jelly when cool, so they can be chopped and served along with the meat. I have suggested using brisket – not the most elegant cut, but excellently flavoured.

serves
8

about 1.5kg (3lb 4oz) brisket, boned
  and rolled
4–6 anchovy fillets
4 cloves
a blade of mace
6–8 peppercorns
120g (4oz) bacon, cut into matchsticks
150ml (5fl oz) red wine
300ml (10fl oz) strong beef stock

4–6 small shallots
1 garlic clove, peeled but left whole
a bouquet garni made from a bay leaf,
  rosemary, thyme and basil
250g (9oz) carrots, trimmed, peeled
  and cut into quarters lengthways
1 pig's foot cut into half lengthways
  (optional)
salt and black pepper

Prepare the beef by unrolling; snip the strings tying it if necessary. Distribute the anchovy fillets over the inside. Pound the spices to powder and sprinkle over. Re-roll and tie again with the seasonings inside.

Take a flameproof casserole that will hold the meat snugly. Add the bacon and let it cook gently until the fat runs. Add the wine and let it boil. Put in the meat, the stock, shallots, garlic and bouquet garni and bring to a simmer. Add the carrots and the pig's foot, if using. Season with 1 teaspoon salt and some pepper.

Cover tightly with doubled greaseproof paper or foil and then the lid of the casserole. Transfer to a low oven, 140°C (275°F, Gas mark 1), and allow to cook for 4 hours. The meat will benefit from being turned once or twice, but it isn't absolutely necessary.

At the end of the cooking time, remove the meat and vegetables to a warm serving dish. Discard the bouquet garni (and the pig's foot, if used). Skim all the fat off the cooking juices. Serve hot with a purée of potato and parsnip to soak up the liquid.

If serving cold: remove the beef, allow it to cool, then store in a cold place; it is better not to refrigerate it unless you have no alternative. Strain the cooking juices, then boil to reduce them by about a quarter. Pour into a bowl, chill and lift off the fat when cold. Remove the strings, carve the meat into neat slices and garnish with the jelly, chopped.

Beef Stew with Root Vegetables & Dumplings

This stew has been a mainstay of English domestic cookery since the mid-19th century. Make it with whatever cut of beef you prefer, cook it with stock or beer and add root vegetables and dumplings. Comfort food for the coldest winter day.

serves
4

50g (2oz) beef dripping, lard or oil, plus a little extra
1 large onion, sliced
2 garlic cloves, peeled and crushed
150g (5oz) turnip, peeled and diced
1 large parsnip, trimmed, peeled and cubed
1 large carrot, trimmed, peeled and cubed
40g (1½oz) flour
450–500g (1lb–1lb 2oz) stewing beef, cut into cubes

250ml (9fl oz) beef stock
250ml (9fl oz) mild beer (optional; use beef stock or wine instead if desired)
1 bay leaf
a few sprigs marjoram, or 1 teaspoon dried marjoram or oregano
salt and black pepper

for the dumplings
1 quantity suet dumpling mix (see page 24) flavoured with horseradish, or mustard and parsley

Heat the dripping in a frying pan or casserole. Fry the onion until translucent, then add the garlic and let it cook a little longer. Remove the mixture from the fat and keep on one side. Fry the root vegetables for a few minutes, then add them to the onions.

Mix 1 teaspoon salt with some pepper and flour and toss the beef into it. Brown the meat in the remaining fat (in batches if necessary – don't overcrowd the pan). Add the meat to the vegetables in the casserole.

Sprinkle the remaining seasoned flour into the frying pan to make a roux (add a little extra fat first if necessary). Add the beef stock, stirring well and scraping any bits of sediment off the base of the pan. Stir in the beer, if using, and bring to the boil. Pour over the meat and vegetables, add the bay leaf and marjoram, then cover. Cook in a gentle oven, 150°C (300°F, Gas mark 2), for about 2 hours.

Make up the dumpling mix.

Remove the casserole from the oven and skim off any excess fat. Taste for seasoning and add more if necessary. Distribute the dumplings over the top. Turn the heat up to 180°C (350°F, Gas mark 4) and return the dish, uncovered to the oven for about 20 minutes, or until the dumplings are cooked through and starting to crisp slightly on top.

Adapt the recipe as desired. If using cuts such as shin of beef or oxtail, reduce the oven temperature to 140°C (275°F, Gas mark 1), and cook for about 4 hours.

Goulash

A dish that was probably introduced to the British repertoire in the early 20th century. This is based on a version that was regularly made by my mother, who came across it as a child when she lived in Bradford, a city with a significant population of immigrants from Eastern Europe between the world wars. She served it with mashed potatoes or rice, but I prefer pasta.

serves 4

60g (2¼oz) bacon, rinds removed, cut into matchsticks
1 medium onion, peeled and finely sliced
20g (¾oz) lard
1 garlic clove, peeled and crushed
450–500g (1lb–1lb 2oz) stewing beef, trimmed and cut into cubes

1 generous tablespoon paprika
1 teaspoon smoked paprika (optional)
400g (14oz) canned chopped tomatoes
salt
sour cream, to serve

Fry the bacon until the fat runs. Remove it to a casserole and put the onions into the bacon fat. Add a little lard if the bacon hasn't yielded much fat. Let the onions cook very slowly until they are quite soft and beginning to yellow. Add the garlic, cook for a minute or two longer, then drain with a slotted spoon and put to one side with the bacon.

Add any remaining lard, turn up the heat and add the beef. Cook it quite fast, stirring frequently, and when the cubes are browned on all sides, sprinkle in the paprika and the smoked paprika (if using). Cook for a couple of minutes longer, stirring all the time, then add the bacon and onions. Stir in the tomatoes and add a teaspoon of salt. Cover tightly and allow to simmer gently for 1½–2 hours.

At the end of cooking time, taste and add more salt if desired. Spoon each portion over some buttered noodles or papardelle and add a spoonful of sour cream to the top. Perhaps not very authentic, but good.

A Welsh Stew

Eliza Acton gave this dish in her book *Modern Cookery for Private Families* (1845). It is recognisably a version of cawl, a soup-like stew of meat and vegetables traditional to Welsh cookery. Acton's version is simple but refined. The better the beef and the stock, the better the end result.

serves
4

about 500g (1lb 2oz) stewing beef, trimmed of any gristle and fat, and cut into slices about 4cm (1½in) square
400ml (14fl oz) beef stock
8 leeks

300g (11oz) small white turnips (or use a slice from a large one)
a pinch sugar
salt and black pepper
chopped parsley, to serve

Put the beef and the stock in a medium-sized flameproof casserole and bring to a simmer. Cover and transfer to a moderate oven, 180°C (350°F, Gas mark 4). Allow to cook gently for 1 hour.

Prepare the vegetables: cut the white part off the leeks, trim and wash and cut into slices about 2cm (¾in) long (this will probably leave quite a lot of green, the best of which can be used for soup). Peel the turnips: small ones can be cut into quarters; if using a piece of a large one, cut as if making chips.

After 1 hour, remove the casserole from the oven. The beef should be fairly tender and the stock well flavoured. Add the prepared vegetables, 1 teaspoon salt, pepper to taste and a pinch of sugar. Return to the oven for about 1¼ hours. Stir occasionally during this time. Check the seasoning and divide between soup plates.

Dust each portion with parsley and serve with floury potatoes, boiled or steamed.

Steak & Kidney Pie

Steak and kidney in puddings or pies had become a classic English combination by the early 20th century. Nicely made and carefully seasoned, they remain one of the best dishes in our traditional repertoire. Earlier versions involved pieces of rump steak and kidney, uncooked, enclosed in suet crust and boiled as a pudding. Later ones evolved to be closer to a highly flavoured beef ragoo covered with puff pastry, as described here.

serves
4

40g (1½oz) dripping
1 large onion, chopped
40g (1½oz) flour, plus extra for dusting
500g (1lb 2oz) stewing beef, trimmed
  and cut into 2cm (¾in) cubes
150–200g (5–7oz) ox kidney, trimmed
  and cut into 1cm (½in) cubes

400ml (14fl oz) beef stock
1 bay leaf
½ teaspoon ground allspice
a little Worcestershire sauce
1 quantity puff pastry (see page 34)
beaten egg, cream or milk, to glaze
salt and black pepper

Melt a little of the dripping in a large frying pan and cook the onion gently for about 30 minutes until soft. Remove to a casserole.

Mix the flour with ½ teaspoon salt and some pepper. Toss the steak and kidney in this. Add the rest of the dripping to the frying pan and brown the meat, in batches if necessary, transferring to the casserole when done. Sprinkle any leftover flour into the frying pan to take up the remaining fat and gradually stir in the beef stock, scraping the base of the pan to incorporate all the juices from cooking the meat. Bring to the boil and cook for a few minutes, then pour it over the meat. Add the bay leaf, allspice and a shake of Worcestershire sauce.

Cover, transfer to the oven and cook at 160°C (325°F, Gas mark 3) for about 2 hours. At the end, taste and add more seasoning as necessary.

Pour into a suitable pie dish and allow to cool. Dust a worksurface with flour, roll out the pastry and cover the pie (see page 35). Decorate with leaves made from pastry trimmings, and glaze with egg, cream or milk. Bake at 220°C (425°F, Gas mark 7) for 20 minutes to raise the pastry, then reduce the heat to 180°C (350°F, Gas mark 4) for a further 15–20 minutes, or until the filling is reheated thoroughly and piping hot.

Lobscouse with Mustard & Parsley Dumplings

Lobscouse is a type of stew made around the coasts of north-west Europe, including the port of Liverpool. And yes, that's why Liverpudlians became known as scousers. Beef, fresh or salted, is the most usual principal ingredient, although fish versions are also known. Dumplings are a good, if non-traditional addition. Tender summer carrots, small white turnips and new potatoes are specified for this summer version; winter vegetables, cubed, work equally well, but give a more robust flavour.

serves
4

500g (1lb 2oz) good-quality
    braising steak
200g (7oz) young carrots, trimmed
    and peeled, halved lengthways
200g (7oz) small white turnips, trimmed
    and peeled, and cut into batons
4 garlic cloves, peeled
a bouquet garni of 1 bay leaf, 1 sprig
    rosemary and a few sprigs thyme

300–400ml (10–14fl oz) water
800g (1lb 12oz) new potatoes, scrubbed
salt and black pepper

for the dumplings
1 quantity dumpling mix (see page 24)
1 teaspoon mustard powder
pinch cayenne pepper
1 generous tablespoon chopped parsley

Trim the meat of any obvious fat and gristle, and cut it into 2cm (¾in) cubes. Put the carrots, turnips and the garlic cloves in a layer over the base of a large pan. Tuck the bunch of herbs in among them. Add the beef in a layer on top. Pour in enough water to cover the vegetables and add the salt and some pepper. Cover tightly with a layer of foil under the lid, and put on the lowest heat. Simmer gently for 1 hour, making sure the liquid doesn't boil away. Then uncover the stew, add the potatoes (cut into halves or quarters if they are large), cover the stew again and continue to cook for about 20 minutes.

Towards the end of cooking, make the dumplings, mixing the mustard, cayenne and parsley into the flour. Uncover the stew, remove the herbs, taste the liquid and add more seasoning if necessary. Drop the dumplings on top of the mixture, re-cover and simmer for another 20 minutes.

Stewed Steak

There are many recipes for stewing or braising steak in English cookery books. They are similar in that they rely on combinations of store-cupboard ingredients – beer, vinegar, and ready-made sauces such as Worcestershire sauce or mushroom ketchup – to produce a strongly flavoured gravy. This is an updated version, which includes a currently fashionable ingredient in the form of balsamic vinegar (but use an inexpensive vinegar, not the costly and precious type). It shares the characteristics of similar recipes from the past, in that it is quick and simple to put together and nice to eat, especially on a cold day.

about 500g (1lb 2oz) braising steak,
    cut into slices about 2cm (¾in) thick
4 garlic cloves, peeled
1 piece of star anise
4 tablespoons soy sauce
2 tablespoons balsamic vinegar
200ml (7fl oz) tomato juice

Put the steak into a shallow ovenproof dish along with the garlic and star anise. Mix together the other ingredients and pour over. Cover the dish with foil and then with a lid if the dish has one. Cook in a low oven, 140°C (275°F, Gas mark 1), for 3 hours, by which time the meat should be extremely tender and surrounded by a well-flavoured sauce. Serve with a mixture of potato and parsnip mashed together.

Braised Ox Cheek
with Wine, Cloves & Oranges

Ox cheek is cheap and well flavoured but needs gentle cooking. This recipe also works with braising steak or escalopes if preferred; shorten the cooking time accordingly. In *The Accomplisht Cook* (1685) Robert May gave a recipe for 'stewed collops of beef', which was the inspiration here and an ancestor of all those dishes of steak braised with wine, beer or the highly seasoned sauces made by commercial sauce manufacturers in the 19th century. The key is strong beef stock: use a home-made one if possible, or a good ready-made one, and reduce it to concentrate the flavour. Really good gravy left from a roast of beef could also be used.

serves
4

600–700g (1lb 5oz–1lb 8oz) ox cheek, cut to give 3–4 thick slices from each one
220ml (8fl oz) red wine
150ml (5fl oz) well-flavoured beef stock

1 orange
6 cloves
scrape of nutmeg
20g (¾oz) flour
20g (¾oz) butter
salt and black pepper

Put the ox cheek in a shallow ovenproof dish. Mix the wine and stock. Remove 4–5 strips of zest from the orange with a canelle knife or a potato peeler and add them, along with the cloves and a generous scrape of nutmeg. Grind in a little black pepper, add about ½ teaspoon salt, and bring the mixture to a simmer. Pour over the beef. Cover tightly with foil and the lid of the dish if it has one. Cook in a low oven, 140°C (275°F, Gas mark 1) or lower if possible, for 3–3½ hours.

Remove the meat to a warm serving dish. Add the juice of half the orange, or more to taste, plus extra salt and pepper as desired.

Knead the flour and butter together and dot over the surface of the sauce, shaking the pan so that it melts into the liquid. The sauce may need to be briefly reheated, but don't overdo it – just enough to thicken it lightly. Serve with a very creamy purée of potato, or plain steamed potatoes.

If using braising steak, it can be cooked for a shorter time at a higher temperature – 1½ –2 hours at 150°C (300°F, Gas mark 2).

Ragoût of Oxtail

2 oxtails, cut into pieces
1 medium onion, finely chopped
2 garlic cloves, peeled and crushed
2 bay leaves, spines removed,
    the remainder finely shredded
1 generous tablespoon chopped parsley
leaves of 3–4 sprigs fresh thyme
600ml (1 pint) red wine
200g (7oz) unsmoked pancetta or
    good bacon, cut into dice

250g (9oz) carrot, trimmed, peeled
    and diced
250g (9oz) mushrooms, finely sliced
1 generous tablespoon truffle paste
    (optional)
500g (1lb 2oz) shallots, peeled
450ml (15fl oz) beef stock
40g (1½oz) flour
40g (1½oz) butter
salt and black pepper

Dissolve 1 tablespoon salt in cold water, then soak the oxtail pieces in it for about 1 hour. Drain well. Put the pieces of oxtail into a deep bowl. Mix the chopped onion, garlic, bay leaves, parsley, thyme, a generous quantity of pepper and the wine, and pour over the meat. Cover and leave to marinate for at least 4 hours.

When ready to cook the stew, take a large flameproof casserole and set it over low heat. Add the pancetta or bacon to the casserole and cook until starting to crisp. Put the carrot and mushrooms on top (no need to stir), and add the truffle paste, if using. Then add the pieces of meat in a layer, and tuck the shallots into the spaces between.

Pour over the marinade, turn up the heat and let it bubble. Add the beef stock and 1 generous teaspoon salt. Bring to the boil, skim well of any scum, then cover the casserole with foil and the lid, and put in a low oven, 140°C (275°F, Gas mark 1). Leave strictly alone for 4 hours.

At the end of the cooking time, remove from the oven and skim off as much fat as possible. Taste and correct the seasoning. Knead the flour and butter together to make a *beurre manié* and dot small pieces of this over the surface of the liquid (remove the pieces of oxtail to a hot serving dish if they seem to be in the way). Heat gently and stir until the sauce has thickened.

Serve with mashed potato, or a purée of potato and celeriac.

Spring Stew of Veal

In summer, English cooks liked to pair veal with fresh greenery and slightly acid flavours. Sorrel was often chosen, but this more unusual combination of cucumbers, lettuce and gooseberries was suggested by Eliza Acton in 1845. She cooked everything together from the start, but the vegetables become very soft this way. Put them in about halfway through cooking so that they retain a little texture.

serves
4

450–500g (1lb–1lb 2oz) stewing veal, cut into 2cm (¾in) cubes
30g (1oz) flour
40g (1½oz) butter
6 spring onions, trimmed, washed and cut into 2cm (¾in) lengths
150g (5oz) green gooseberries
350ml (12fl oz) veal or chicken stock

½ cucumber, peeled, seeds removed and the flesh cut into 1cm (½in) dice
2 Little Gem lettuces, outer leaves removed, trimmed, washed and cut into quarters lengthways
salt and black pepper
chives, to garnish

Toss the veal in the flour. Melt the butter in a frying pan or flameproof casserole. Add the veal and fry briskly to brown. Add the spring onions and gooseberries and continue to fry for a few minutes. Stir in any remaining flour, then add the stock, stirring well to make a sauce. Add ½ teaspoon salt and a little pepper. Cover well and simmer gently for about 1 hour, stirring occasionally.

Add the cucumber and lettuce. Cover and cook for a further 1 hour, or until the meat is tender and the vegetables cooked. Stir, check the seasoning, and garnish with a scatter of chopped chives. Serve with new potatoes.

Veal & Ham Pie

serves 4–6

400–500g (14oz–1lb 2oz) veal,
  preferably from the loin or leg
100–150g (3½–5oz) cooked ham in
  one piece
2 hard-boiled eggs
1 generous tablespoon chopped parsley
leaves from a few sprigs winter
  savoury or thyme, chopped
15–20 large leaves of fresh basil,
  torn into pieces
2 bay leaves, spines removed and
  the leaves shredded
pinch cinnamon
120ml (4fl oz) well-reduced
  stock – veal for preference,
  otherwise chicken

salt and black pepper
1 quantity puff pastry (see page 34)
flour, for dusting
beaten egg, cream or milk,
  to glaze

for the forcemeat
200g (7oz) spinach, well washed
200g (7oz) breadcrumbs made
  with fresh white bread
50g (2oz) fat bacon (unsmoked),
  cut into small pieces
½ teaspoon salt
1 egg

Cut the veal, ham and hard-boiled eggs into thin slices. Mix together the parsley, winter savoury or thyme leaves, half the basil leaves and the bay leaves. Add the cinnamon, salt and pepper. Toss the veal pieces in this and put on one side.

Put the spinach in a pan; the only water it will need is that left on the leaves from washing it. Put it over medium heat with a lid on. Stir until wilted, then tip it into a sieve and press well to remove excess water. Put it together with the breadcrumbs, bacon, remaining basil leaves and salt into a liquidiser or food processor, then blend to a paste. Add the egg and process just enough to mix.

Take a deep pie dish and put a layer of ham in the base. Cover this with some of the forcemeat. Add the slices of hard-boiled egg, then more forcemeat, then the veal, interspersed with any remaining forcemeat. Pour in the stock.

Roll out the pastry and cover the dish (see page 35). Glaze with beaten egg, cream or milk. Cook at 220°C (425°F, Gas mark 7) for 20 minutes, reduce to 180°C (350°F, Gas mark 4) and cook for a further 45 minutes to 1 hour.

Veal Olives

These thinly rolled slices of veal were often used as pie fillings in the 17th and 18th centuries, but they are very good on their own with a little sauce. The name has nothing to do with olives but is derived from an old French word for lark: the little meat rolls, plumply stuffed, are reminiscent of small birds lying in the dish.

Mace, a popular spice in the 18th century, is best bought whole; crush it to a powder with a mortar and pestle just before using. The recipe can be used with beef olives as well — omit the Parma ham and use red wine and beef stock as the cooking liquids.

serves 4

4 veal escalopes, each weighing
    approximately 100g (3½oz)
2 slices Parma ham
100g (3½oz) breadcrumbs
50g (2oz) butter, plus a little extra
    for frying
2 anchovies
leaves of 3–4 sprigs thyme

zest of ½ lemon, finely grated
about ½ teaspoon ground mace
1 small egg
200g (7oz) button mushrooms,
    trimmed and sliced
120ml (4fl oz) dry sherry
120ml (4fl oz) veal or chicken stock
salt and black pepper

Lay the escalopes on a plate or board and cover each one with a slice of Parma ham. Put the breadcrumbs in a bowl. Melt the butter and crush the anchovies into it. Pour into the breadcrumbs, add the thyme, lemon, mace and some black pepper. Mix in the egg, stir well, divide into four and spread each portion over the ham on top of the escalopes. Roll up, enclosing the stuffing, and tie each olive with thread in two or three places.

Melt a little butter and fry the olives briefly, just enough to brown lightly. Remove to a plate, and add the sliced mushrooms to the pan. Fry over fairly high heat, stirring well until they brown a little. Put the rolls of meat back in, pour in the sherry and let it bubble, then add the stock. Bring to a simmer, cover and transfer to a moderate oven, 150°C (300°F, Gas mark 2) for 1 hour.

Serve with plain boiled rice.

Lamb & Mutton

MEAT FROM SHEEP was hugely important for both rich and poor in the past. Lamb meant young animals – anything from house lambs, which were early season sucking lambs a few weeks old, to animals consumed in the late summer or early autumn following their birth. Mutton meant adult sheep, often several years old. Lamb, especially young lamb, was a delicacy; mutton, while often very good, was more workaday fare. It was ubiquitous and cuts for stewing were comparatively inexpensive.

Recipes for lamb in fricassées appeared in the 17th century, and leg of mutton *à la daube*, *à la braise* or in ragoo in the French-influenced cookery of the 18th century. A native tradition of mutton dishes also flourished. Flavours from maritime environments were used: capers, samphire, anchovies and oysters were all added to sauces or garnishes. Mutton was used in pies and sometimes added to Christmas plum porridge (try the recipe on page 45 with lamb, omitting the sugar and replacing the currants, raisins and prunes with an equivalent weight of dried apricots).

Less extravagant mutton dishes were also numerous. By the 19th century a combination of mutton and potatoes had become established in English food. Lancashire hotpot is said to have originated from the cotton towns of south-east Lancashire. It is a good-tempered dish that can be left to cook gently for a long time, a product of a mill-based work culture in which women required recipes that cooked in the low heat of a dying fire while they were out of the house.

Cawl, which sometimes uses mutton, is an everyday dish of Welsh cookery (see A Welsh Stew, page 53, for a beef version). It is more liquid, between a soup and a stew, and includes many vegetables. Irish Stew (see page 72) was a dish that could be left on gentle heat for a long time, to be ready when required. Another mutton and potato combination is Shepherd's Pie. It is a recipe the English managed to export to India during the colonial period, and it has continued to evolve there (see page 76).

Cooking Stews & Pies
with Lamb or Mutton

TODAY, MOST SHEEP meat that arrives on the market is described as lamb, a convention I have followed here, although the animals concerned are often well on their way to adulthood. Mutton is difficult to buy and generally comes from ewes. It is impossible to find the mutton known in the past, which came from well-fattened wethers about four or five years old. The fine distinctions once made between these meats are no longer available to us – but nor is the poor-quality, strongly flavoured and stringy mutton sometimes remarked upon, so perhaps we should be grateful.

All lamb is relatively tender. Even cuts that appear lean, such as leg, can be cut up for stews, but they are expensive and are more usually used for roasting. 'Stewing lamb' usually indicates meat from the neck – best end, middle or scrag. Best end is most elegant and is relatively expensive, as it often gets used as a rack of lamb for roasting. Middle and scrag are less easy to find than previously. Scrag may seem unpromising, containing a lot of bone and fat, but like all neck of lamb cuts, it has an excellent flavour. It also produces good stock as it cooks, something on which the homely mutton and potato dishes depend. Shoulder of lamb, usually sold in the past as a whole or a half for roasting, can be found as smaller pieces, as steaks or sometimes as 'henrys' (quarters), good for using in stews. If desired, the meat can be cut off the bones. Lamb shanks, usually cut from the leg, but sometimes from the shoulder, are excellent for stewing.

Cuts such as neck and shanks must be cooked very slowly for about 3 hours, allowing the large amounts of collagen they contain to soften and gelatinise, adding body to the dish so that the flavours develop and permeate sauces. Potatoes absorb some of the fat contained in the meat. Shoulder steaks and better-quality lamb, diced, can be cooked on higher temperatures for shorter times (about 1½ hours in a moderate oven).

The distinctive and strong flavour of lamb responds well to many treatments. Root vegetables, especially onions, carrots and turnips, make a good basic stew such as Haricot of Lamb (see page 74), or in the style used for simple beef casseroles (see Beef Stew with Root Vegetables, page 48). Flavours from maritime environments are also excellent, as in Lamb Stewed with Samphire, Capers and Artichokes (see page 86).

Irish Stew

Comfort food. A simple, inexpensive dish known in the cookery of Ireland and Britain since at least the mid-19th century. Irish Stew was originally made in a pan, cooked gently on top of the stove, and often considered better if some of the potatoes began to dissolve into the mixture, thickening it. The best stews were said to be made with the minimum of water or stock. Cooking in the oven means it can be left to look after itself – but put it in a pan and simmer on the very lowest heat on the hob if preferred. It has a gentle, mild flavour; if you find it bland, try adding the mixture suggested at the end.

serves 4

300g (11oz) onion, peeled and coarsely chopped

1kg (2lb 4oz) neck of lamb (middle or scrag), cut into chops

300g (11oz) small white turnips, trimmed, peeled, halved and cut into slices lengthways

1.2kg (2lb 11oz) potatoes, peeled and cut into large dice

salt and black pepper

300ml (10fl oz) stock (lamb for preference)

to garnish (optional)

a handful of fresh coriander leaves

1 small garlic clove, peeled

1 fresh hot green chilli, to taste

a little finely grated lemon zest

Take a large casserole (or pan) and build the meat and vegetables in layers, beginning with the onion and following with the meat, turnips and potatoes, then repeating until the ingredients are used up. Sprinkle on 1 teaspoon of salt and some pepper between the layers. Bring the stock to the boil, pour over the meat and vegetables and cover with buttered foil or paper and the lid.

Cook in the oven, 180°C (350°F, Gas mark 4), for at least 2 hours, or longer on a lower temperature, if desired. A stew simmering on the hob will need checking occasionally to make sure it isn't drying out.

At the end of cooking, taste, correct the seasoning, and serve straight from the pot. To garnish, chop the coriander leaves, garlic and green chilli fairly finely, stir in the lemon zest and scatter a little of this mixture over each portion.

Harrico of Mutton or Lamb

The word haricot (or harrico) is derived from French *harigoter*, meaning 'to cut up'. It meant a stew or ragoo, but got confused with the usage of haricot as a name for beans in French, and sometimes led English cooks to think that haricot of mutton included beans. This summery version doesn't, but by all means add some fresh French beans towards the end of cooking time.

This recipe is based on one given by Anne Cobbett in her book *The English Housekeeper* (1851). She evidently considered the basic recipe bland and added proprietary sauces popular in the mid-19th century. I've suggested Thai fish sauce, which adds a salty note. For the stock, use lamb or chicken stock, simmered with turnip, carrot, onion and parsley to strengthen the flavour.

serves 4

500–600g (1lb 2oz–1lb 5oz) lamb or mutton – best end of neck, loin or chump chops
30g (1oz) butter
400ml (14fl oz) strong stock
4–6 small young carrots, trimmed, peeled and cut into quarters lengthways
a bunch of spring onions, washed, trimmed, and cut into 3–4cm (1¼–1½in) lengths
200g (7oz) small white turnips or kohlrabi, peeled and cut into sticks
4 celery sticks cut into 3–4cm (1¼–1½in) lengths
15g (½oz) flour
salt and black pepper

to season (optional)
cayenne pepper
Worcestershire sauce
Nam pla (Thai fish sauce)

Trim the chops of any excessive fat. Melt half the butter – around 15g (½ oz) – in a large frying pan and brown the chops on both sides. Add the stock, bring to the boil and simmer gently for 45 minutes. Add the vegetables and continue to cook gently for another 15–20 minutes. By this time, the meat should be tender. Season carefully. A pinch of cayenne, following Anne Cobbett's example, is a good addition, as are about 1 teaspoon of each of the sauces. If using these, remember that they are salty, and add them before finally tasting and adding any more salt and pepper.

Knead the remaining butter with the flour and drop into the stew in small pieces. Heat gently until boiling, shaking to distribute the butter through the liquid so that the sauce thickens. Serve with new potatoes, and other vegetables as desired.

Bolton Hotpot

oysters – as many as you like or can afford, up to 20 (optional)
50g (2oz) beef dripping
1 large onion, peeled and thinly sliced
2 garlic cloves, peeled and crushed
800g–1kg (1lb 12oz–2lb 4oz) middle neck of lamb, cut into chops
30g (1oz) flour
400ml (14fl oz) stock, preferably lamb

2 lamb's kidneys, cored and cut into slices
pinch ground allspice
250g (9oz) mushrooms, sliced fairly thinly
900g (2lb) potatoes, peeled and sliced
a little butter
salt and black pepper

If using oysters, open them first, or ask the fishmonger to do so. Strain and reserve any liquor they contain to remove stray bits of shell or grit.

Melt the dripping in a frying pan and add the onion. Cook fairly briskly until it is starting to yellow. Add the garlic, stir well, cook for a moment longer, then drain and remove the onions to a large deep casserole or other ovenproof dish. Put the chops into the hot fat and brown on both sides, then put these on top of the onions.

Sprinkle the flour into the fat left in the pan and stir to make a roux. Stir in the heated stock to make a sauce. Add 1 generous teaspoon salt and plenty of pepper. Allow it to cook gently for a few minutes. Put the kidneys on top of the chops and dust them with a little allspice. Follow this with the sliced mushrooms in a layer, then the oysters, if you are using them. Add the oyster liquor if there is any, and pour over the sauce from the frying pan. Put the potatoes on top, ending with a nice neat layer of large overlapping slices. Dot with small pieces of butter.

Cover with the lid of the casserole and cook at 180°C (350°F, Gas mark 4) for about 2½ hours. Then uncover the pot, turn the heat up to 200°C (400°F, Gas mark 6), and cook for another 20 minutes or so to brown the top layer of potatoes.

Pickled red cabbage is the traditional accompaniment to hotpot in Lancashire.

Indian Shepherd's Pie

serves
4

3 tablespoons oil

3 cloves

3 cardamom pods

1 large onion, peeled and very finely
    chopped

4 garlic cloves, peeled and crushed

2cm (¾in) cube of fresh root ginger,
    peeled and grated

1 teaspoon cumin seed, toasted in a
    warm frying pan and then ground

1 teaspoon coriander seeds, ground

½ teaspoon turmeric

pinch chilli pepper, or to taste

450–500g (1lb–1lb 2oz) minced lamb

2 large tomatoes, peeled and chopped

100ml (3½fl oz) water

½–1 teaspoon garam masala

salt and black pepper

1 tablespoon chopped mint

for the topping

900g (2lb) potatoes, peeled
    and cut into chunks

100ml (3½fl oz) milk

40g (1½oz) butter

2 tablespoons chopped
    coriander leaves

1 fresh mild green chilli,
    finely chopped

chilli powder or hot fresh chilli
    (finely chopped), to taste

salt and black pepper

Heat the oil in a large frying pan. Add the cloves and cardamom and allow them
to heat through, then add the onion. Fry gently, stirring frequently, until it is
beginning to brown evenly – this will take at least 20 minutes.

Add the garlic and ginger and continue to cook for 1–2 minutes, then add the
cumin, coriander and turmeric, plus a pinch of chilli pepper. Stir well to heat the
spices, then add the minced lamb. Keep stirring it and breaking up any lumps
until the meat is lightly browned and the onion mixture is well amalgamated with
it. Add the tomatoes and the water, then turn the heat down low, cover, and allow
the mixture to simmer for a minimum of 1 hour, or 2 hours if possible. Stir from
time to time and add a little water if it shows signs of drying out. At the end of
cooking time, stir in a little garam masala, salt to taste and the chopped mint.
Pour the mixture into an ovenproof dish, then remove the cloves and the
cardamom pods.

To make the topping, boil the potatoes, drain and mash with the milk and butter, adding salt to taste and quite a lot of black pepper. Stir in the coriander leaves and the mild chilli; add a little chilli powder or hot chilli to taste.

Spread the mashed potato over the meat mixture, roughening the surface with a fork. Bake in the oven at 190°C (375°F, Gas mark 5) for about 25–30 minutes, or until the potato is browning, or chill and reheat later, allowing about 40–45 minutes and making sure the pie is properly heated through.

Lamb Meatballs

Recipes for meatballs appear in early English recipe books from the end of the 16th century until the middle of the 18th century. They were highly seasoned and enhanced with whatever spices, dried fruit and nuts happened to be fashionable at the time. This version is loosely based on recipes from the early 18th century.

serves 4

400g (14oz) minced lamb
50g (2oz) fresh white breadcrumbs
1 garlic clove, peeled and crushed
1 tablespoon very finely chopped parsley
1 tablespoon finely chopped basil
½ teaspoon nutmeg
1 egg
30g (1oz) pistachio nuts, blanched (optional)

2 rashers fatty bacon (unsmoked), diced
10–12 small shallots, peeled
150ml (5fl oz) red wine
150ml (5fl oz) good stock, beef for preference
2 teaspoons cornflour, slaked with a little water
salt and black pepper

Put the lamb, breadcrumbs, garlic, herbs, nutmeg, 1 teaspoon salt, pepper to taste, and the egg into a large bowl. Mix well, a task best done by kneading all together by hand.

Divide the mixture into 20, and form each piece into a small ball (wet your hands in cold water to stop it sticking). If using pistachio nuts, seal one or two in the centre of each little ball. Heat a deep frying pan or shallow flameproof casserole and add the bacon pieces. Fry gently until they have yielded most of their fat. Add the peeled shallots and the meatballs and let them cook gently, turning occasionally until the meatballs have browned on all sides.

Pour in the wine and let it bubble, then add the stock. Cover and cook gently for 30–45 minutes. Then stir in the cornflour mixture, heating gently and stirring all the time until the sauce thickens. Taste and correct the seasoning if necessary. Serve with plain boiled rice or mashed potato and a salad of bitter leaves.

Sunflower Oil / Groundnut
Garlic -
Ginger - Fry Hard - Brown Edge

~ King Prawns
- Chillies (Dutch Red NO. 6)
Kaffir Lime Leaves
Sugar (Brown)
Lemon Grass few slices
Coconut Cream
Fish Sauce
chopped Roasted Peanuts
Thai Basil or Basil

NHS APP
Couch to 5K

WHOLE HAZELNUT IN MILK CHOCOLATE AND NUT CROQUANTE

INGREDIENTS: **MILK** CHOCOLATE 30% (SUGAR, COCOA BUTTER, COCOA MASS, SKIMMED **MILK** POWDER, CONCENTRATED **BUTTER**, EMULSIFIER: LECITHINS (**SOYA**), VANILLIN), **HAZELNUTS** (28.5%), SUGAR, PALM OIL, **WHEAT** FLOUR, WHEY POWDER (**MILK**), FAT-REDUCED COCOA, EMULSIFIER: LECITHINS (**SOYA**), RAISING AGENT (SODIUM BICARBONATE), SALT, VANILLIN.

SUITABLE FOR VEGETARIANS

STORE IN A COOL DRY PLACE

DISTRIBUTED BY: FERRERO UK Ltd, 889
GREENFORD ROAD, GREENFORD,
UB6 0HE, UK.
VISIT US AT www.ferrero-range.com

BES

Braised Lamb Shanks

Lamb shanks usually remained attached to roasts of lamb until the early 1980s, at which point a change in fashion liberated them to become foundations for dishes in their own right. Slowly cooked in rich, savoury sauces, they have become a modern British classic.

4 lamb shanks
2 tablespoons olive oil, plus extra
    for frying
300ml (10fl oz) red wine
salt and black pepper
1 medium–large onion, peeled
    and chopped finely
2 garlic cloves, peeled and
    chopped finely

the leaves from 1 sprig rosemary,
    peeled and chopped finely
1 generous tablespoon flour
a bouquet garni of a few sprigs
    each of parsley, marjoram,
    mint and basil plus 2 strips
    of orange zest
about 150ml (5fl oz) lamb or
    beef stock

Put the lamb shanks in a suitable bowl and add the oil, wine, 1 teaspoon salt and some pepper. Cover and leave the meat in the marinade for at least 2 hours (overnight is better). Turn the meat in the mixture occasionally. When ready to cook, drain the meat from the marinade, reserving the marinade for the sauce.

Heat a little olive oil in a flameproof casserole. Add the onion, garlic and rosemary and fry briskly, stirring frequently, until it is just beginning to turn golden. Pat the meat dry, toss it in the flour and add to the mixture, turning well until lightly browned. Dust in any remaining flour. Pour in the marinade, stir well and bring to the boil, stirring well. Add the bouquet garni and the stock and return the mixture to the boil.

Cover the pot with foil and then with the lid. Transfer to the oven at 150°C (300°F, Gas mark 2) and cook for 2½–3 hours. At the end of cooking time, taste the sauce and add more seasoning if necessary.

Serve with mashed potato, jacket potatoes or Stovies (see page 211).

Lamb Korma

This is a recipe written down by Colonel Kenny-Herbert in the late 19th century in his book *Culinary Jottings for Madras* (1885). This 'quoorma', as he spelt it, is a reminder that curry in the 19th century was not always a mixture of cold meat re-hashed with a stock curry powder. I make no apology for lifting his recipe almost exactly as he detailed it because it is excellent, but have halved the quantity of butter – the 4oz (120g) originally suggested seemed a little too much.

serves 4–6

about 700g (1lb 8oz) leg of lamb, fillet
    end for preference
50g (2oz) fresh root ginger, peeled
    and grated
1 teaspoon salt
50g (2oz) butter
2 medium onions, peeled and
    sliced
2 garlic cloves, peeled and
    finely chopped

spice mixture – made from 1 teaspoon
    coriander seed, 1 teaspoon black
    peppercorns, ½ teaspoon cloves
    and ½ teaspoon cardamom seeds
    ground together
150ml (5fl oz) single cream
100g (3½oz) almonds, blanched
1 dessertspoon turmeric
1 teaspoon sugar
the juice of 2 limes

Cut the meat into neat pieces about 2cm (¾in) square, discarding any bone and fat. Put the pieces in a bowl with the grated ginger and salt, then stir well and leave to marinate in a cool place for about 2 hours.

Melt the butter in a heavy flameproof casserole. Add the onions and garlic and cook gently until they begin to turn light gold – this will take about 30 minutes. Then add the meat mixture and fry, turning frequently, until well browned.

Stir in the spice mixture and continue to cook gently for a few minutes. Warm the cream to almost boiling and put it with the almonds into a blender. Whizz together to reduce the almonds to fragments, then press through a sieve; use a little water to help the process if the mixture is very thick. Stir the almond-flavoured cream into the meat along with the turmeric and sugar. Place over the lowest possible heat and cook gently for 40 minutes. Stir frequently, making sure it doesn't stick. Add a little water as necessary. Check to make sure the meat is cooked through, then stir in the lime juice.

Shoulder of Lamb with Pearl Barley & Winter Vegetables

A dish that takes its inspiration from two traditions – firstly the habit of stewing or boiling joints of meat, common in the English kitchen until the mid-20th century; and secondly the idea of using flavours associated with the vegetable-heavy broths of Scottish cookery.

serves 4–6

1 large leek, trimmed and washed
2 large carrots, trimmed and peeled
½ medium celeriac, washed and peeled
60g (2¼oz) pearl barley
about 6 sprigs thyme and 6 sprigs
    parsley, tied in a bouquet

½ large shoulder of lamb
500ml (18fl oz) water or light chicken
    or beef broth
salt and black pepper
fried breadcrumbs (see page 30)

Select a casserole or stew dish that will hold the ingredients neatly. Slice the leek and the carrots into pieces about 1cm (½ in) thick, and cut the celeriac into cubes the same size, then put them in the casserole. Add the pearl barley and put the herbs on top. Place the joint of lamb over this, season all with 1 generous teaspoon salt and some pepper. Bring the water or broth to the boil and pour into the dish. Cover well with foil and the lid of the dish if it has one. Cook in a low oven, 140°C (275°F, Gas mark 1), for about 4 hours.

At the end of the cooking time, remove the covers and skim off any excess fat. Prepare the fried breadcrumb mixture.

To serve, remove the meat from the casserole and cut into neat slices or bite-sized pieces, discarding any large pieces of fat or gristle. It should be very tender. Give each person a share of the vegetables, barley and broth topped with some of the meat and scatter the breadcrumb mixture over. Serve with a dish of cabbage and some floury boiled potatoes.

Lamb's Liver with Orange

Liver gained a bad reputation in British cookery, probably through school meals when it was served cooked to a texture like shoe leather. If stewed gently with plenty of seasonings until just cooked, it is very different.

serves
4

about 30g (1oz) fat – lard
    or beef dripping
1 large onion, peeled and
    thinly sliced
1 garlic clove, peeled and crushed
400g (14oz) lamb's liver, cut into
    thin slices

20g (¾oz) flour
zest of ½ orange, finely grated; and
    the juice of the whole orange
about 150ml (5fl oz) strong
    beef stock
a pinch of chilli powder
salt and black pepper

Melt the fat in a frying pan. Fry the onion and garlic gently until transparent, then remove them with a slotted spoon and put on one side. Dust the liver with flour and fry lightly on both sides. Stir any remaining flour into the fat, then add the onions and garlic back to the pan. Stir in the orange zest and juice, the stock, a small pinch of chilli powder, 1 scant teaspoon salt and a generous grind of black pepper. Stir well, then cover and cook on a low heat.

Test after 5 minutes by inserting the end of a sharp knife into one of the liver slices – if the juices run very red, cook for another 5–10 minutes. It's nicest if the meat is just cooked. Taste and add more seasoning if desired.

Serve with a bowl of fluffy mashed potato.

Lamb Stewed with Samphire, Capers & Artichokes

Recipes using flavours derived from maritime environments appear in cookery books from the 17th century onwards. Here is one inspired by dishes mentioned by Jos Cooper in *The Art of Cookery Refin'd and Augmented* (1654) and Robert May in *The Accomplisht Cook* (1685). Use mutton if it is available: this was a dish for meat with depth of flavour. Samphire is a plant with fleshy, brilliant green stems. It grows on salt marshes, which are often used for grazing sheep, and is available from fishmongers from late May until September. It is a winter food and habitat for certain birds, so always check that it is sustainably harvested.

Fresh artichokes can be used if available: buy four, trim away the tops of the leaves, remove the thistly choke from the centre and boil for a few minutes until tender, then add them to the stew.

serves 4

2 tablespoons olive oil
1 small onion, peeled and finely chopped
1 garlic clove, peeled and crushed
about 750g (1lb 10oz) lamb or
    mutton chops, loin, chump
    or best end of neck
1 tablespoon flour
100ml (3½fl oz) red wine
1 anchovy, either salted or preserved in oil

150ml (5fl oz) beef stock or water
a little nutmeg
100g (3½oz) samphire
30g (1oz) salted capers
100–125g (3½–4½oz) globe artichokes
    preserved in oil – drained weight
salt and black pepper
chopped parsley, to serve

Heat 1 tablespoon olive oil in a frying pan or flameproof casserole and add the onion and garlic. Cook gently, stirring frequently, until soft and golden. Remove with a slotted spoon.

Trim any excess fat off the chops, then coat lightly with the flour. Add the remaining olive oil to the pan and fry them on either side until lightly browned, then sprinkle in any remaining flour and stir well. Still stirring, add the wine and let it come to the boil, then add the anchovy and stock or water. Mix well and bring to a simmer. Grate in a little nutmeg and add a couple of turns of black pepper. Cover and simmer very gently or put the casserole in a moderate oven, 180°C (350°F, Gas mark 4), for about 45 minutes, or until the meat is tender.

Rinse the samphire and pick over, discarding any soft or discoloured bits. Rinse the capers free from salt, and drain any oil from the artichokes. Cut these into quarters if this has not already been done.

When the meat is cooked, skim off any excess fat. Add the samphire, capers and artichokes to the stew, stir gently, and return to the oven for 5–10 minutes, just long enough for the samphire to cook and the capers and artichokes to heat through. Taste and add salt if necessary, but this is unlikely because the capers and anchovy will provide plenty.

Dust with parsley and serve with new potatoes.

Pork

PORK CASSEROLES are something of a rarity in English cookery, but pig meat still went into many stews. As lardons or as rashers wrapped round other meats, bacon gave fat and flavour to lean cuts of meat, poultry and game. It remains a vital ingredient giving an underlying, salty savouriness to stews in the grand tradition of ragoos and braises.

Ham was also used. Essence of ham was essential to fashionable kitchens in the 18th century: it was made by cutting a raw ham into slices, which were stewed with root vegetables, veal stock, mushrooms, truffles and spices. Eventually it was strained and the liquor kept for adding to other dishes. Hams were also braised. According to John Nott, in his *Cook's Dictionary* (1726), these were served hot with a ragoo of veal sweetbreads, chicken livers, cockscombs, mushrooms and truffles, or even sometimes crayfish.

Clearly, pork was valuable as a preserved meat: fine hams graced the tables of the rich; soused or collared pork was stored up by careful housewives; and innumerable barrels of salt pork were carried in the stores of sailing ships. Farmers and cottagers grew pigs on to bacon weight and salted as much as possible of the meat. Bacon goes much further than fresh pork to add savour to otherwise bland food, something well known to the less wealthy. Friedrich Engels, observing the lives of industrial workers in the 1840s in Manchester, noted how the poorest used small amounts of bacon to flavour the potatoes that were their staple food; a lack of this small resource was symptomatic of total destitution.

Probably because of its usefulness as preserved meat, fresh pork was unusual in stewed dishes in English cookery. Small cuts of pork, such as loin chops, seem to have been grilled for preference. Maybe pork stews simply fell through a social black hole – not smart enough to go into cookery books, too simple or commonplace to be noted elsewhere. That said, there is little evidence of poorer people stewing pork, except as faggots – a type of meatball made from pork meat and offal braised in stock, a dish of the rural tradition.

Cooking Pork in Pies & Stews

WHEN COOKING PORK, a certain amount of fat distributed through the meat is desirable. Lean cuts such as leg or loin tend to be dry. Shoulder meat or spare rib chops (cut from the roasting joint, not the rack of ribs) are the best for stews. Belly pork, cut into large dice or used in one piece for braising (see page 94) is also a possibility, but do remove the skin (which can be added to the braising liquid) and trim off any excess fat before cooking. A pig's trotter is also a good addition to Beef à la Mode (see page 46).

Apples and apple drinks are often used with pork. Cider is often cited as a cooking liquid: English ciders can be assertive in flavour, so go cautiously with it or mix with apple juice. White wine or verjuice make good substitutes. Pork shares to some extent the pale, mild qualities of veal and works well in some recipes originally intended for the latter. These are quite numerous in early cookery books.

Bacon for stews needs to be a traditionally produced dry-cured variety, not too lean. After all, what is required is fat and flavour, which is more concentrated in dry-cured meat. Pancetta can be used instead, and is often easier to buy as ready-cut lardons or in a thick slab that can be cut up as needed. Always use unsmoked meat unless otherwise stipulated. When choosing ham, fat is less desirable, but similar rules about dry curing and lack of smoke apply. A handful of bacon or ham lardons fried until crisp and then drained well enhance many stews; try them to garnish some of the fish recipes such as Haddock, Leek and Potato Stew with Mussels (see page 188) or Sarah's Summer Vegetable Stew (see page 209).

English fresh sausages are quite different from those of European countries, and the variety of those made by craft butchers has expanded way beyond the boundaries of English tradition in the past 20 years. It is worth trying them out in a pulse-based casserole – for instance, with lentils in a sauce (see page 104).

Belly Pork Braised with Cider

Belly pork is usually cooked by roasting, but it is good rolled around a seasoning of herbs, braised gently and served cold – better than leaner cuts that tend to be dry. Choose the meat carefully, looking for a reasonable but not excessive layer of fat on top. Ask the butcher to remove the skin and bones, but take them home for the stock.

serves
6

about 1kg (2lb 4oz) piece of belly pork, skin and bones trimmed and reserved
generous pinch chilli powder
1 teaspoon fennel seeds, bruised
2 tablespoons finely chopped parsley
leaves from 6–8 sprigs thyme

2 garlic cloves, cut into slivers
zest of 1 lemon
15g (½oz) lard
200ml (7fl oz) cider
200ml (7fl oz) stock (preferably beef)
salt and black pepper

Put the pork, fat side down, on a board. Sprinkle with salt and grind a generous quantity of black pepper over it. Scatter with the chilli powder, fennel seeds, parsley, thyme, garlic and lemon zest. Roll up and tie firmly. The pork can be left overnight if desired.

When ready to cook, heat the lard in a flameproof casserole that will hold the meat neatly. Brown on all sides, then pour in the cider and let it bubble. Add the stock and bring to a gentle simmer. Tuck the skin and bones down beside the meat. Cover and transfer to a moderate oven, 160°C (325°F, Gas mark 3), for 2½–3 hours, by which time the pork should be very tender.

Remove from the cooking liquor and allow it to cool a little. Wrap in greaseproof paper, put between two boards and press lightly – a 900g (2lb) weight or a couple of cans of tomatoes on top is adequate. Leave until cold. Taste the cooking liquor and season if necessary. Strain into a bowl and chill, then remove any fat from the top. The stock should set to a jelly.

To serve, cut the pork into very thin slices. Chop the jelly and use it as a garnish. Serve with a salad of mixed leaves tossed in a mustardy dressing.

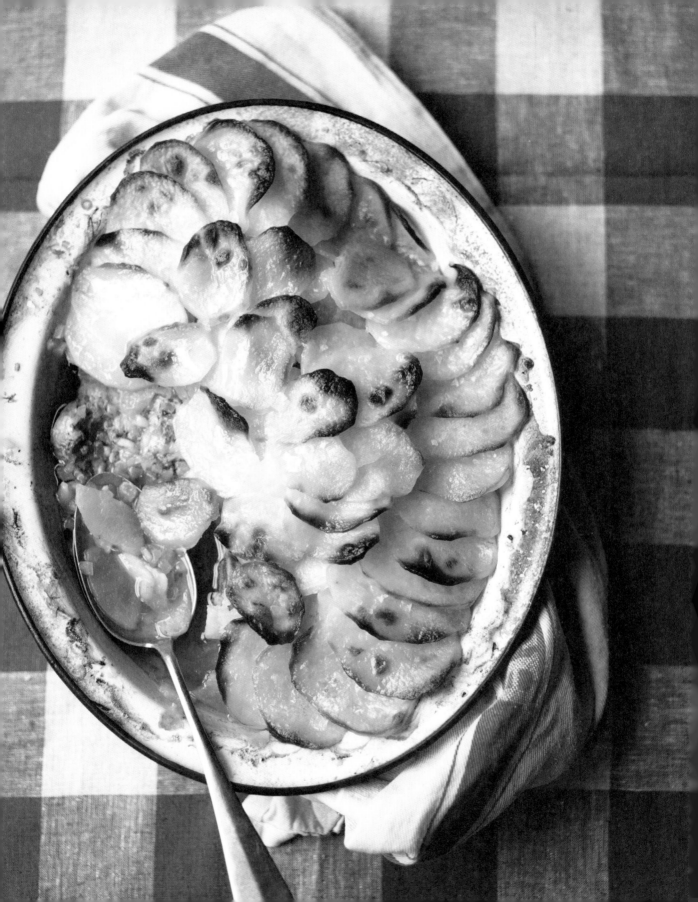

Pork with Potatoes & Apples

This is really a pork version of a hotpot. Verjuice is the juice of unripe grapes and is available bottled from some delicatessens. It has a subtle sour-sweetness, good with all sorts of rich meat. If it is unavailable, a mixture of white wine and lemon juice in the proportions of about 3:1 is the best substitute. Use a potato peeler to peel off the lemon zest.

serves 4

4 spare rib pork chops, total weight about 800g (1lb 12oz)
1 medium onion, peeled
2 garlic cloves, peeled
8 juniper berries
a strip of lemon zest

2 eating apples – Cox or russet for preference
120ml (4fl oz) verjuice
800g–1kg (1lb 12oz–2lb 4oz) potatoes
about 20g (¾oz) butter
salt

Put the meat in a deep ovenproof pie dish or casserole. Chop the onion, garlic, juniper berries and lemon zest together until quite fine. Mix with the pork, add salt, then cover and leave to marinate for 2 hours.

Peel and core the apples, then cut them into thin slices. Layer over the pork. Pour in the verjuice. Then peel the potatoes and slice them thinly as well. Use them to cover the pork and apples, sprinkling lightly with salt and dotting with butter as you go. Cover the top with buttered greaseproof paper or foil and cook in a low oven, 140°C (275°F, Gas mark 1), for 2 hours. At the end of this time, turn the heat up to 200°C (400°F, Gas mark 6), remove the cover and allow the top layer of potatoes to brown and crisp.

Normandy Pork Stew

This is a variation on the idea of the Harrico of Mutton (see page 74). The original recipe was given by Eliza Acton (1845). Loin chops work well with the new potatoes in this recipe.

serves
4

500–600g (1lb 2oz–1lb 5oz) pork chops from the loin or spare rib
1 tablespoon flour
20g (¾oz) butter or oil such as sunflower
300–400ml (10–14fl oz) light pork or chicken stock
4 spring onions, washed, trimmed and tied in a bunch with some parsley stems

500–600g (1lb 2oz–1lb 5oz) small new potatoes, scrubbed or scraped as preferred
salt and black pepper
chopped parsley, to garnish

Trim the chops of any excess fat. Mix the flour, 1 teaspoon salt and some pepper, and dust the chops with it. Heat the butter or oil in a large frying pan and brown the chops on both sides.

Sprinkle in any leftover flour and stir to amalgamate with the fat. Stir in the stock and bring to the boil. Add the spring onions and the parsley stems. Cover, reduce the heat and allow the stew to simmer very gently for 30–45 minutes. At the end of this time, add the potatoes in a single layer on top of the meat. Cover and continue to cook for about 30 minutes, or until the potatoes are tender.

Remove from the heat, fish out the bunch of parsley stems and spring onions and discard them. Allow to settle for a few minutes, then skim off any excess fat. Check the seasoning and adjust if necessary. Scatter a little chopped parsley over each portion.

Faggots

Faggots are little bundles of pork meat and offal, wrapped in caul fat (a transparent membrane laced with fat, which lines the abdominal cavity of pigs and other meat animals). They belong to the now-extinct rural tradition of pig killing, and in the first half of the 20th century became the food only of the poor. Recipes for them underwent a certain amount of innovation, when the idea of the gastropub first evolved in the late 1990s. This is my own updated version.

serves
4 – 6

200g (7oz) boneless pork such as loin steaks – try to buy some with a reasonable amount of fat, about 25% of the total

200g (7oz) pork liver

200g (7oz) stewing veal

100g (3½oz) bacon, rinds removed

1 generous tablespoon chopped parsley

1 generous teaspoon chopped marjoram

1 generous teaspoon thyme leaves (lemon thyme if possible)

2 large garlic cloves, peeled and crushed

100g (3½oz) shallots, peeled and finely chopped

1 teaspoon salt

2 tablespoons brandy

zest of 1 lemon, finely grated

a piece of caul fat from a pig

300ml (10fl oz) strong stock from pork, chicken or beef

black pepper

Mince the pork, liver, veal and bacon together and put in a bowl. Add all other ingredients except the caul fat and stock. Season with pepper. Mix with your hands to make sure everything is evenly distributed. Divide the mixture into 18–20 equal pieces and form into balls.

Put the caul fat into a bowl of tepid water for a few minutes. Carefully unravel it to give a large sheet. Use kitchen scissors to cut it into small pieces, about 8cm (3¼in) square, avoiding any bits that are very fatty. Drain the pieces and wrap each ball of faggot mixture in one, trimming any excess caul.

Put the faggots in a baking dish that holds them neatly. Pour the stock around them, and bake in a moderate oven, 180°C (350°F, Gas mark 4) for about 1 hour. They should be cooked through and the tops nicely browned. At the end of cooking time, pour off the cooking juices (keep the faggots warm in a low oven), allow the fat to rise and skim off as much as possible. Then reheat to boiling, pour back around the faggots and serve.

Pork with Apple Juice & Quinces

Pork and apples go well together, whether it's because the pigs have been feeding on windfalls in an orchard or the meat has been cooked with apples or their products. This recipe uses apple juice but replaces the more usual sliced apples in the sauce with quinces – a related species, but with a distinctive perfumed aroma. Use a potato peeler to peel off the lemon zest.

serves 4

30g (1oz) butter
4 pork spare rib steaks, total weight
    about 800g (1lb 12oz)
2cm (¾in) length of cinnamon stick,
    ground
8 cloves, ground
1 teaspoon peppercorns, ground
a thumb-sized piece of fresh root
    ginger, peeled and cut into thin
    matchsticks

3–4 strips lemon zest
350ml (12fl oz) apple juice
1 dessertspoon soft brown sugar
1 large or 2 small quinces, cut into
    quarters, the pips and core removed
about 1 teaspoon salt

Melt the butter in a flameproof casserole and brown the pork on both sides. Remove it and keep to one side. Add the ground spices, the ginger and the strips of lemon zest to the residual butter and cook gently, stirring all the time, for 3–4 minutes. Then pour in the apple juice, bring to the boil and cook until the liquid has reduced by about a third.

Stir in the brown sugar, add the pork steaks and the quinces. Add the salt. Seal, covering the dish with foil and the lid, if it has one. Put in the oven at 140°C (275°F, Gas mark 1) and cook for about 2 hours, or until the pork is tender.

Serve with a mixture of potatoes and parsnips mashed together.

Pork Meatballs with Saffron Sauce

This recipe was inspired by a dish of small pear-shaped meatballs, which appears in several cookery books of the late 17th and early 18th centuries. The original was based on veal, but the recipe works well with pork. The egg yolk and lemon juice thickening gives the sauce a pleasing acid note, good with the rich meat.

serves
4

400g (14oz) minced pork
50g (2oz) fresh white breadcrumbs
leaves from 3–4 sprigs thyme
1 generous tablespoon finely
   chopped parsley
zest of 1 lemon, and the juice
   of ½ lemon

about ¼ teaspoon ground cloves
2 eggs, separated
pinch of saffron threads
300ml (10fl oz) stock, pork
   or chicken for preference
sage leaves and stems, to serve
salt and black pepper

Put the pork, breadcrumbs, thyme, parsley, lemon zest, cloves, 1 scant teaspoon salt and some pepper in a large bowl. Add the egg whites. Mix well and divide into 16 portions. For an authentically 17th-century look, roll into pear shapes, wider at one end than the other.

Heat a deep frying pan or a flameproof casserole. Add the saffron strands and let them toast gently for a moment – only enough to release their fragrance; don't let them burn. Pour in the stock and bring to the boil. Add the meatballs and simmer gently, turning two or three times, for 30–45 minutes.

Just before serving, beat the egg yolks with the lemon juice. Remove the meatballs to a warm serving dish. Off the heat, pour the egg and lemon mixture into the sauce. Heat very gently, stirring all the time, until the sauce has thickened a little and is thoroughly hot. Taste, correct the seasoning and pour around the meatballs. Garnish each 'pear' with a sage leaf and stem.

Serve with plain boiled rice.

Sausage & Lentil Stew

The fresh sausages of British tradition often lack the robustness and seasoning power of their European cousins, but are still good with lentils, echoing the long-time combination of pork with pulses. A well-made Cumberland sausage, meaty and highly peppered, is good for this recipe. If properly made, it should arrive coiled up in a long piece, rather than formed into links. Cut into suitable lengths before cooking.

serves 4

1 tablespoon lard, goose fat or olive oil
1 medium onion, chopped fairly finely
leaves from 3–4 sprigs rosemary,
    chopped
4 garlic cloves, peeled and chopped
600–700g (1lb 5oz–1lb 8oz)
    good-quality pork sausages

200ml (7fl oz) red wine
300g (11oz) small green lentils
    or Puy lentils
400ml (14fl oz) water
1 tablespoon Dijon mustard
salt and black pepper

Heat the fat or oil in a heavy frying pan or flameproof casserole. Add the onion, rosemary and garlic and cook briskly, turning frequently, until the onion begins to brown in patches. Add the sausages and allow to cook gently, turning every so often so that they brown a little.

Pour in the wine and let it bubble, then add the lentils, water and some black pepper. Bring to the boil, transfer to a casserole, cover and put into the oven at 160°C (325°F, Gas mark 3).

Cook for about 30 minutes, then check progress. If the lentils seem to be drying out, add a little more water, preferably boiling. Return to the oven for another 20–30 minutes, after which the lentils should be soft but still holding their shape. Mix the mustard through the casserole, then taste and check the seasoning – the sausages will probably have made the mixture salty enough, but add a little more as necessary.

Serve with a salad of watercress or other sharp leaves, and some good bread.

Chicken &
Other Poultry

CHICKENS WERE, and still are, the most commonplace of domestic fowl. If the table needed something extra they were one of the first things available. In previous centuries cooks knew how to deal with everything from the youngest, most tender birds to tough old hens. Capons, turkeys, ducks and other tame birds also provided meat for the pot.

Methods for stewing and braising all sorts of domestic fowl are common until the end of the 19th century, when, except for those used with chicken, they seem to have gone into decline. Chicken fricassées were popular but the birds were also good in complicated ragoos and braises, simpler more homely stews, or rustic pie fillings with ham or herbs or cream. Chicken has been a meat of choice for making curries ever since Hannah Glasse published 'To make a Currey the India Way' in *The Art of Cookery Made Plain and Easy* (1747); it is the first known recipe.

There are plenty of recipes for stewing or braising turkeys. Even if they were smaller than our Christmas birds, with added stuffing, stock, beef, veal, ham and vegetables a braised turkey must have needed skill and confidence on the part of the cook. Whole boned turkeys were stuffed with forcemeat to make galantines or put into thick raised crusts for pies to be kept and sent some distance.

Eighteenth-century cooks were fond of cooking ducks with ragoos, or *à la braise*, but duck with peas (sometimes a simple roast duck with boiled green peas, sometimes an elaborate braise with peas cooked *à la française*) and duck with turnips are two dishes they knew which constantly recur over the years. Both make good combinations, which is why they are still regarded as part of the traditional English repertoire.

Cooking Poultry in Stews & Pies

FOR THE BEST FLAVOUR, buy the best and most carefully reared birds you can find. This goes for all poultry, but is especially true for chickens. It can't be said too often that they will taste better, their meat will have a firmer texture and their bones will make better stock.

It is unusual now to braise or stew a chicken or other bird whole, although there is no reason why it shouldn't be done. But a chicken cut into joints or taken off the bone cooks more evenly, it is easier to serve and eat, and portions are easy to buy. Chicken for stewing or for pies generally looks neater if skinned; add the skin to the stockpot. Unless featuring a mature boiling fowl (a possibility now that keeping hens has become a popular hobby), a chicken stew cooks relatively fast: allow 1–1¼ hours for a small bird, but do check carefully to make sure the meat is adequately cooked. A whole bird might take a little longer, especially if large, and an older fowl should be allowed 2 hours at a slow simmer.

The light fresh flavours of spring and summer vegetables and herbs go well with the meat (see Fricassée of Chicken and Asparagus, page 118). Slightly acidic flavours such as white wine and lemon juice work well, or try richer creamy sauces as in Turkey Fricassée (see page 130), or wild mushrooms (see Chicken and Wild Mushrooms in a Potato Case, page 112).

Making stews with turkey is easier than it used to be. Formerly, one would have to buy the entire bird and cut it up, but turkey portions and diced turkey have taken the trouble out of this. Like chicken, it is important that the meat is fully cooked; also, meat from turkey legs needs time – allow about 1½ hours gentle stewing to make it tender. Apart from the recipes given on pages 126–130, turkey can be used in recipes for chicken; or try escalopes cut from the breast as an alternative to veal in Veal Olives (see page 65) or Veal and Ham Pie (see page 64); and turkey mince instead of pork in Pork Meatballs with Saffron Sauce (see page 103), adding a light spicing of cayenne or chilli pepper – don't overdo it; a generous pinch is enough.

Duck, a darker, denser meat, is delicious cooked gently in rich stews. I've added flavours taken from East Asian cookery to update the 18th-century notions of Stewed Duck with Green Peas (see page 132) and Duck with Turnips (see page 131). For a more conventional dish of the *à la braise* type, try using duck in the recipe for Compôte of Pigeons (see page 145). Like other poultry, duck is now available in quarters or joints. If you don't want to cook a whole bird, use legs, and leave duck breasts for grills or other quickly cooked dishes.

Chicken & Wild Mushrooms in a Potato Case

The idea for this recipe came from another of Colonel Kenny-Herbert's recipes, in this case the suggestion of serving *chicken à la financière* in small drum-shaped cases made of deep fried potato. Chicken cooked this way, is, as the name suggests, a rich production and the original requires large quantities of truffles. Though still quite complex to make, this recipe is more modest. If the idea of the enclosing potato case is daunting, serve the stew separately, with the mash baked in a buttered dish and scattered with the crumbs and cheese as an accompaniment.

serves
4

1 chicken weighing about
    2–2.5kg (4lb 8oz–5lb 8oz)
1 carrot, trimmed and peeled
1 onion, peeled
1 celery stick
a bouquet garni of a bay leaf, some
    thyme and some parsley stems
10g (¼oz) dried porcini mushrooms
30g (1oz) butter
50g (2oz) pancetta (unsmoked),
    cut into matchsticks
400g (14oz) mushrooms (about half
    ordinary button mushrooms and the
    rest, if possible, wild ones such as
    chanterelles), washed and trimmed

30g (1oz) flour
100ml (3½fl oz) dry sherry
salt and black pepper

for the case
1.5kg (3lb 4oz) floury potatoes,
    peeled and cut into chunks
4 egg yolks
1 teaspoon salt
½ teaspoon mace
20g (¾oz) butter
20g (¾oz) breadcrumbs, made
    from stale bread
20g (¾oz) grated Parmesan

Begin with the chicken. Joint it, and cut the meat from the breasts and thighs into neat cubes about 1.5cm (⅝in) square. Cover the meat and keep in the fridge. Put the bones and the skin in a pan with the carrot, onion, celery and the bouquet garni. Cover with water, bring to the boil and simmer gently for about 2 hours to make a good stock (use the wings and drumsticks for another dish, or add them to the stock pot).

Strain off the stock, skim off as much fat as possible, then return 500ml (18fl oz) of it to a clean pan. Put this over gentle heat and allow it to reduce to about one-third of the original volume. This will be needed for the stew.

When ready to make the stew, put the dried mushrooms in a small bowl and add about 100ml (3½fl oz) boiling water. Then melt the butter in a frying pan and add the pancetta. Allow to cook gently until the fat is transparent. Remove and set aside. Slice the mushrooms and fry in the fat from cooking the bacon, cooking quite briskly and stirring frequently until they begin to brown. Drain and add to the pancetta.

Dust the chicken meat with flour and fry in the same pan, turning until lightly browned on all sides. Sprinkle in any remaining flour, stirring to absorb any fat in the pan, then add the sherry and let it bubble. Stir in the porcini and their soaking liquid, plus the fried mushrooms and pancetta. Add the reduced stock and mix well. Allow to cook very gently for about 30 minutes, by which time the chicken pieces should be well done. Taste and add salt and pepper as necessary.

For the potato case, boil the potatoes and mash (without additions). They are best passed through a ricer, a sieve or a mouli-legumes to make sure they are perfectly smooth. Beat in the egg yolks, salt and the mace, then return to the pan and stir them over a low heat for a few minutes to dry the mixture out a little.

Take the tin or dish and use some of the butter to coat the inside. Use two-thirds of the potato mixture to line the base and sides, covering them as evenly as possible and making sure there are no gaps or thin patches through which the stew can escape. Pour in the stew, ensuring that it doesn't come above the level of the potato lining. Carefully dot the rest of the potato over the top, then use a fork to spread it evenly across to form a lid and seal the edges. Melt the remaining butter and stir into the breadcrumbs. Add the Parmesan and sprinkle this mixture over the top of the potato.

Bake at 200°C (400°F, Gas mark 6) for about 25 minutes, until the top is golden brown and the stew thoroughly hot. Unmould on to a deep dish if you feel brave; otherwise, serve from the cooking dish.

Chicken in Red Wine

This recipe, based on the French *coq au vin*, is reminiscent of rich, meaty 18th-century ragoos and chickens cooked *à la braise*. True *coq au vin* is difficult to make properly without the vital ingredient – a cockerel weighing in at several kilos, with richly flavoured dense meat that needs slow cooking; however, a good free-range chicken and careful preparation and seasoning gives a delicious stew, well worth the effort.

serves 4 – 6

150g (5½oz) fat bacon or pancetta (unsmoked), cut into 1cm (½in) dice

about 16 small shallots or button onions, peeled

250g (9oz) mushrooms (small open ones with dark gills are best)

about 20g (¾oz) butter

a chicken weighing about 2kg (4lb 8oz), cut into 8 joints

1 medium onion, peeled and chopped

1 medium carrot, trimmed, peeled and chopped

4 garlic cloves, peeled and crushed

100ml (3½fl oz) brandy

1 bottle red wine (Burgundy for preference)

1 bay leaf

3–4 sprigs thyme

1 teaspoon concentrated beef stock

salt and black pepper

Fry the diced bacon or pancetta until most of the fat has been given up and the pieces are quite crisp. Remove them with a slotted spoon and put to one side. Put the button onions in the fat and fry until they colour a little. Add them to the bacon pieces. Fry the mushrooms until the tops turn gold in patches and add them to the bacon and onions. Add the butter to the remaining bacon fat and fry the chicken pieces, skin side down, until gold. Put these to one side.

Add the chopped onion, carrot and garlic to the fat in the pan and cook briskly, stirring frequently, until the onion begins to turn gold. Warm the brandy in a ladle, ignite it and pour it into the pan, stirring well. When the flames have died down, pour in the red wine. Add the bay leaf, thyme and the concentrated stock, bring to the boil, and allow to cook rapidly until reduced by half.

Remove the herbs, allow the sauce to cool a little and blitz it to a purée in a blender or food processor. Transfer it to a casserole. Add the chicken pieces, the mushrooms, onion and bacon, a generous grind of black pepper and ½ teaspoon salt. Cook in the oven for 40 minutes at 180°C (350°F, Gas mark 4), stirring halfway through. At the end of this, check to make sure the thickest parts of the chicken joints are fully cooked (if they are still a little pink, cook for a few more minutes). Taste and add more salt if desired.

A bowl of pasta, with a knob of butter and a tablespoon of finely chopped parsley stirred through, makes a good accompaniment to this dish.

Fricassée of Chicken & Asparagus

serves
4

1 chicken weighing about 1.5kg
    (3lb 4oz)
zest and juice of 1 lemon
leaves of 4–6 large sprigs fresh thyme
1 tablespoon chopped parsley
30g (1oz) butter
1 small onion, peeled and finely
    chopped

1 generous tablespoon flour
250ml (9fl oz) good chicken stock
2 bunches asparagus, washed, the
    woody ends of the stems discarded
    and the rest cut into pieces about
    2cm (¾in) long
75ml (3fl oz) single cream
salt and black pepper

Cut the legs away from the body of the chicken and divide them into thigh and drumstick. Cut the breasts and wings off the bird. Divide each in two, leaving a portion of breast meat attached to each wing. Trim the tips off the wings. Skin the joints, putting the skin and carcass in the stockpot.

Mix together the lemon zest and juice, thyme and parsley. Grind in a generous amount of black pepper. Put the chicken into this mixture, turn it to coat well, then cover and leave to marinate for at least 2 hours (overnight if possible). Stir the meat around in the marinade from time to time.

To start the fricassée off, melt the butter in a frying pan and cook the onion gently until transparent. Lift it out and put it into a flameproof casserole or large pan. Remove the chicken from the marinade (reserve any remaining juices). Dust the joints with flour and brown them lightly in the butter used for frying the onions. Add them to the casserole or pan. Add any remaining flour into the frying pan, stir well to mop up any fat, and add about two-thirds of the stock and any leftover marinade. Stir well, scraping up any residues from frying and bring to the boil. Season with ½ teaspoon salt and pour over the chicken. Cover, and simmer over a very low heat for about 1 hour, or until the chicken pieces are cooked through. If it seems to be drying up, add a little more stock, but don't overdo it.

Allow the stew to cool a little and skim off any excess fat. Then add the asparagus and return to the heat for 5–10 minutes, until the asparagus is just cooked. Add the cream, stir gently and heat through. Taste, adjust the seasoning and serve with new potatoes or rice.

Chicken & Leek Pie

Chicken makes an excellent pie filling. In the traditions of the English kitchen, it is often combined with ham, as is veal; mushrooms are another common addition. Leeks are less usual, but make a good winter pie.

serves
4

1 chicken
50g (2oz) flour, plus extra for dusting
scrape of nutmeg
50g (2oz) butter
a piece of lean ham or gammon,
   weighing about 200g (7oz),
   cut into about 1cm (½in) cubes

4–6 leeks (depending on size), white
   part only, washed and cut into
   1cm (½in) lengths
300ml (10fl oz) chicken stock
1 quantity puff pastry (see page 34)
beaten egg, cream or milk to glaze
salt and black pepper

Joint and skin the bird as directed in Fricassée of Chicken and Asparagus (see page 118).

Season the flour with ½ teaspoon salt, some pepper and a good scrape of nutmeg. Dust the chicken joints with the mixture. Melt the butter in a large frying pan and brown the chicken lightly in it. Put the cubed ham or gammon into the base of a suitable pie dish. Put the chicken on top, and then the sliced leeks.

Stir any remaining flour into the butter left in the pan, then stir in the chicken stock. Bring to the boil, stirring all the time, and cook for a few minutes. Taste to check the seasoning and add a little more if necessary. Pour this into the pie dish as well. Allow to cool a little.

Cover the pie with the pastry (see page 35). Decorate with pastry leaves, as taste and fancy suggest, and glaze with beaten egg, cream or milk.

Bake in a hot oven, 220°C (425°F, Gas mark 7), for 20 minutes to set the pastry, then reduce the heat to 180°C (350°F, Gas mark 4) and cook for a further 45–50 minutes until the pastry is golden and the filling cooked through.

Chicken with Prunes & Saffron Broth

A simple but well-flavoured light stew based loosely on the Scottish cock-a-leekie, which involves a chicken and a piece of beef cooked in broth with prunes and leeks. I've omitted the beef and leeks from this recipe. Use a good-quality chicken; this can be cooked whole in the broth and carved afterwards if desired, but it is easier to handle if cut into joints.

serves
4

12 ready-to-eat prunes
2 tablespoons whisky (optional)
400ml (14fl oz) strong chicken stock
12 whole peppercorns
a pinch of saffron threads

1 sprig parsley
1 chicken, about 1.5–2kg (3lb 4oz–4lb 8oz), cut into four joints
salt

The evening before you want to make the stew, put the prunes into a small bowl with the whisky and turn them around in it. If you don't want to use whisky, omit this step and proceed as below.

When ready to cook, put the stock into a large pan and add the prunes plus any whisky they haven't soaked up, the peppercorns, saffron and sprig of parsley. Bring to a simmer, add the chicken pieces, season with 1 scant teaspoon salt and cover. Simmer gently for 30–40 minutes, or until the chicken pieces are cooked all the way through.

Serve each joint in a deep plate, adding a generous amount of broth and two or three prunes to each helping. Boiled floury potatoes, or potatoes mashed with cooked leeks are good accompaniments to the stew.

Chicken & Tomato Stew

A recipe derived from a stew my mother sometimes made. She used it for the hens from her poultry flock which had passed their prime, becoming what she called 'boiling fowl'. They were not as tender as chickens, but had lots of flavour.

serves
4–6

50g (2oz) butter or 4–5 tablespoons
    sunflower oil
1 large onion, finely chopped
2–3 garlic cloves, crushed
leaves from 1 sprig rosemary,
    chopped
30g (1oz) flour

1 large chicken, preferably
    free-range, about 2kg
    (4lb 8oz), skinned and
    jointed into 10–12 pieces
250ml (9fl oz) white wine
6–8 plum tomatoes, or 400g
    (14oz) canned tomatoes
salt and black pepper

Heat the butter or oil in a large frying pan. Add the onion, garlic and rosemary and fry briskly, stirring frequently, until the onion begins to form pale golden patches. Use a slotted spoon to transfer it to a casserole.

Season the flour and use to dredge the chicken pieces, then fry gently until golden in the fat used for frying the onion. Add the chicken pieces to the casserole.

Sprinkle any remaining flour into the pan and stir well, then pour in the white wine and keep stirring, scraping any up residues from the base of the pan. When the mixture has come to the boil, add it to the casserole.

If using fresh tomatoes, put them in a bowl, cover with boiling water for a couple of minutes, then drain them and peel off the skins. Cut each one in half, and add to the casserole. Canned tomatoes can be added as they are, straight from the tin, including the juice.

Cover and cook at 180°C (350°F, Gas mark 4) for about 1½ hours. Taste and correct the seasoning. Serve with steamed or mashed potatoes, or rice.

Chicken Curry

serves
4

1 chicken or chicken portions, about
    1.5–2kg (3lb 4oz–4lb 8oz)
3 small onions, peeled and sliced
    (add the onion skin and trimmings
    to the stock)
1 carrot, trimmed and peeled
1 celery stick
a few black peppercorns
2 garlic cloves, peeled
1 dessertspoon turmeric
1 dessertspoon coriander seed, ground
1 teaspoon cayenne pepper

1 teaspoon sugar
1 teaspoon salt
2cm (¾in) cube of fresh root ginger
juice of 1 lime
50g (2oz) butter
about 1 tablespoon flour
1 heaped tablespoon curry powder
1 teaspoon ground cinnamon
150ml (5fl oz) coconut milk
1 bay leaf
1 tablespoon mango chutney
green coriander, to garnish

Joint the chicken and remove the skin. Cover the meat and refrigerate. Put the skin and chicken carcass in a stockpot with the onion skins, carrot, celery and black peppercorns, cover with water and simmer to make stock.

While this is cooking, make a seasoning paste: take one of the onions, one garlic clove, the turmeric, coriander, cayenne, sugar, salt and ginger and process them together in a blender. Add a little of the lime juice if it seems dry.

Melt the butter in a large pan. Dust the chicken pieces lightly with flour and fry until pale gold. Drain and set aside. Add the sliced onions and remaining garlic clove (crushed) and fry briskly. Stir frequently and cook until golden. Stir in the curry powder and allow to cook for a moment, then add the seasoning paste and cinnamon. Fry gently for a few minutes before stirring in about 150ml (5fl oz) chicken stock and 100ml (3½fl oz) coconut milk. Simmer for 15 minutes. Next add the bay leaf, the chutney and the remainder of the lime juice. Add the chicken pieces, bring to the boil and simmer very gently until the chicken is tender and cooked through – about 45 minutes, depending on the size of the pieces. Stir occasionally and add a little more stock if it shows signs of drying out.

Once the chicken is cooked, stir in the remaining coconut milk. Taste and adjust the seasoning if necessary. Garnish with coriander leaves and serve with rice.

Braised Turkey & Celery with Tarragon Dumplings

The combination of turkey and celery is a neglected classic of the English kitchen. Maybe this is because 19th-century versions requiring a whole boiled turkey and a sauce based on several heads of celery look daunting, but the combination works well in a less grand manner.

serves 4

20g (¾oz) butter
4 small shallots, peeled and
    finely chopped
400–500g (14oz–1lb 2oz) turkey
    thigh, diced
20g (¾oz) flour
2–3 sprigs lemon thyme
zest of ½ lemon
about ½ teaspoon ground mace
400ml (14fl oz) strong turkey or
    chicken stock
salt and black pepper

½ head celery trimmed and cut into
    2cm (¾in) lengths

for the dumplings
120g (4oz) plain flour, plus a little
    for dusting
80g (3¼oz) white breadcrumbs
1 teaspoon baking powder
a generous pinch salt
100g (3½oz) suet
1 tablespoon chopped tarragon
about 200ml (7fl oz) water

Melt the butter in a heavy frying pan. Add the shallots and cook gently for about 10 minutes, or until translucent. Toss the turkey meat in flour and fry until the outside is lightly coloured. Add the thyme, lemon zest and mace, then stir in the stock. Season with 1 scant teaspoon salt and a little pepper and add the celery. Bring to a simmer, transfer to a casserole, cover and cook in the oven at 160°C (325°F, Gas mark 3), for about 1 hour.

Towards the end of this time, make the dumpling mixture: put everything except the water in a bowl and mix well. Add the water gradually, stirring until it forms a soft, slightly sticky dough (add a little more water if necessary). Dust a board and your fingers with flour and form the dough into about 18–20 dumplings.

By now, the meat should be just cooked but not yet tender. Skim off any excess fat, taste and season. Put the dumplings on the stew and return to the oven, uncovered, for another 20–30 minutes, or until they are crisp on top and golden.

Daube of Turkey

Daube is a word now applied to a dish of meat and vegetables braised slowly. This old-fashioned dish of French farmhouse cookery uses specially shaped pots, which are bulbous with narrow necks. They hold the ingredients in layers and the small opening cuts down on evaporation. Any deep pot will do. Ask the butcher for a piece of pork rind – this adds body and richness to the sauce. Chorizo is not traditional, but goes well with turkey.

serves
4

turkey breast steaks, weighing about
    100–125g (3½oz–4½oz) each
a thin rasher of bacon for each steak
100g (3½oz) pork rind, cut in
    small pieces
1 medium onion, peeled and
    finely chopped
4–6 small shallots, peeled and
    finely chopped
1 medium carrot, peeled and
    cut in small dice

1 beef tomato, skin and seeds
    removed, flesh diced
1 clove garlic, peeled and crushed
100g (3½oz) chorizo sausage, cut
    in thick slices
a bouquet garni of a piece of leek,
    celery, 1 bay leaf, a few sprigs
    of thyme and parsley and a strip
    of orange zest
400ml (14fl oz) white wine
salt and black pepper

Wrap each piece of turkey in a rasher of bacon. Blanch the pork rind by putting it in a small pan, adding boiling water and cooking for 2–3 minutes. Drain it. Mix the onion, shallot, carrot, tomato and garlic together.

Put the pork rind into the pot and add a layer of vegetables. Put the chorizo sausage on top and scatter more vegetables over. Put the bacon-wrapped turkey steaks on top of this and add the bouquet garni. Season with some pepper and about ½ teaspoon salt (the sausage and bacon will also be salty, so be cautious). Cover with the remaining vegetables and pour in the wine.

Put the lid on the pot with a layer of foil underneath to make it airtight. Transfer to a low oven, 140°C (275°F, Gas mark 1) for 2½–3 hours.

This can be eaten hot or allowed to cool in the pot and for gentle re-heating. If the sauce seems thin, pour some into a small pan and reduce by fast boiling before returning it to the stew.

Turkey Fricassée

A simple, soothing dish using the wine-flavoured creamy sauce typical of fricassées of the late 18th and early 19th centuries. Truffle paste can be bought in small jars and, while not cheap, is a relatively inexpensive method for adding concentrated mushroom flavour to dishes of this type.

serves
4

20g (¾oz) butter
500g (1lb 2oz) turkey breast meat, cut
    into strips
1 garlic clove, peeled but left whole
60–80ml (2–2¾fl oz) white wine
60–80ml (2–2¾fl oz) single cream

2 generous teaspoons truffle paste
2 teaspoons butter kneaded
    with 2 teaspoons flour
salt and black pepper
chopped parsley, to garnish

Melt the butter in a frying pan that has a lid. Add the turkey meat and brown lightly on both sides. Put in the garlic clove, then stir in the wine and let it bubble. Season with ½ teaspoon salt and some black pepper. Cover, reduce the heat and allow the mixture to cook gently for about 10 minutes or until the meat is done. Remove the garlic.

Stir in the cream and bring back to the boil for a couple of minutes. Add the truffle paste and stir well. Check the seasoning. Dot the flour and butter mixture over the surface of the sauce and shake the pan so that it melts in and thickens it slightly (it may not all be needed).

Garnish with chopped parsley and serve with rice or pasta.

Duck with Turnips

Another combination that appeared in cookery books of the early 18th century, given a 21st-century lift with seasonings derived from Chinese cookery. Once again, it needs really well-flavoured stock for the best results. It is nicest made with small white turnips (the flat ones are very pretty), but a piece from a large one can be used.

1 duck
flour, for dusting
30g (1oz) butter
1 small onion, peeled, halved and
   finely sliced
1 tablespoon finely grated fresh
   root ginger
4 cloves, beaten to a powder
1 piece star anise

350ml (12fl oz) stock – beef or duck
8 small white turnips, peeled and
   quartered, or a piece taken from
   a large turnip, weighing about
   500g (1lb 2oz) peeled and cut into
   neat dice
1 tablespoon arrowroot
salt and black pepper

Cut the duck into joints and dust them with flour. Melt the butter in a frying pan or flameproof casserole and put the duck in, skin side down. Allow it to cook slowly until the skin develops golden brown patches, then turn and brown the other side. Remove to a plate.

Using the fat in the casserole, add the onion and cook gently until it becomes soft and golden. Add the ginger and stir well, then stir in the cloves and add the star anise. Return the duck to the pan, pour in the stock and add the turnips. Add 1 scant teaspoon salt and some pepper.

Allow to simmer gently for 45 minutes to 1 hour. Once the pieces of duck are just cooked through, remove them to a warm plate. If the contents of the pan seem excessively fatty, skim well. Mix the arrowroot with a little cold water and stir it into the cooking juices. Bring back to the boil and cook, stirring, until the sauce thickens slightly. Taste, adjust the seasoning and serve.

Stewed Duck with Green Peas

Recorded from the early 18th century onwards, stewed duck and green peas became a classic of English summer food. Success depends on good stock, which must be well flavoured. If in doubt about this, start with about half as much again, add a little onion, carrot, parsley and some mushroom trimmings and allow it to reduce gently to the amount required. Beef stock or gravy was always specified for this dish.

serves 4

30g (1oz) butter
1 duck, jointed, or 4 duck joints
flour, for dusting
100g (3½oz) pancetta or bacon
    cut into matchsticks
8 small shallots, peeled and halved
2 tablespoons brandy
a bouquet garni of parsley, thyme,
    1 bay leaf and 1 sprig mint
zest of ½ lemon, cut into thin strips
3–4 cloves, pounded to a powder
a pinch of cayenne

350ml (12fl oz) well-flavoured
    beef stock
200g (7oz) frozen peas
4–6 spring onions, trimmed
    and finely sliced
leaves from 6–8 sprigs mint, finely
    chopped – about 1 generous
    tablespoon
leaves from 6–8 sprigs basil,
    torn into shreds
salt

Melt the butter in a wide pan. Dust the duck with flour, then brown slowly on both sides in the butter. Remove from the pan; pour off the fat.

Return the pan to a low heat. Spread the pancetta or bacon and shallots over the base. Put the duck on top, then pour in the brandy and let it bubble. Add the bouquet garni, lemon zest, 1 scant teaspoon salt, the cloves and cayenne. Pour in the stock, bring to a simmer and cover. Let the mixture stew very gently for about 1 hour. Towards the end of this time, test the duck meat to see if it is cooked – the juices should run clear. When done, transfer the pieces to a serving dish. Discard the bouquet garni. Skim off the excess fat.

Return the pan with the cooking juices to the heat. Add the peas and spring onions and bring to the boil. Season if necessary. As soon as the peas are done, remove from the heat, stir in the mint and basil and serve with a bowl of little new potatoes.

Game Birds

WILDFOWL OF MANY species found their way on to the table in the past, but the range we consider edible has now narrowed – no more herons on the dinner table. It is further limited by the availability of some species. Pheasants, which are bred in huge numbers for shoots, and partridges are the most easily available, along with some wild duck species. Also described as game birds are pigeons, once kept as domestic poultry but now more likely to be wild wood pigeons; and quail, which were always wild birds in the past but now generally come from farmed stock.

Many methods for cooking game birds were suggested over the centuries. Stews for them were unusual in 17th-century books, although they were boiled and presented in vast heaps as an 'olio' on the tables of the rich.

Statements of wealth were made less obviously as fashions changed in the 18th century, and game birds were cooked *à la braise*. Partridges were highly valued for their fine flavour, and stock made from them was part of the culinary arsenal of the early 18th-century French cooks. The birds, if not to be roasted, might be cooked gently with cabbage, or stuffed with a breadcrumb-based forcemeat and stewed in highly flavoured sauces or braised.

Domestic pigeons provided a ready source of meat all year round. They were raised in specially built dove or pigeon cotes, often large and impressive structures; several can be seen at National Trust properties. Squabs (young birds) and older birds were both eaten, cooked in many different ways. Jugging (cooking in a tightly sealed pot that stood in another vessel full of boiling water) was a method used for the older birds, or they were stuffed with rich forcemeats, or put into fricassées or ragoos. Wood pigeons were, presumably, also eaten, although little distinction seems to have been made between the two in cookery books. Quail were just one of any number of small birds that were presented at the table, the rest of which – larks, wheatears, plovers – we would never now consider as food.

Any of these birds could be made into a pie, sometimes as a method of short-term preservation, sometimes as a dish for that day's dinner. Pigeon pie, like rabbit pie, acquired a certain status as the icon of a way of rural life which people supposed had existed before modern life swept it aside in the 20th century. A proper game pie was made with a raised crust, to be eaten cold, but pies to be eaten hot were also made.

Cooking Game Birds in Pies & Stews

BECAUSE OF THEIR ASSOCIATIONS with hunting and landed estates, game birds have always had high status. Despite the abundance of pheasants wandering the country lanes, this past glory still clings to them, and they are given a certain amount of deference in the kitchen. Stewing was usually relegated to a method for cooking older birds, and it was the leftovers of roasts that were converted to hashes and little-made dishes.

The meat of all these birds is lean, although cooking in a sauce counteracts dryness. In the past, birds were generally larded and cooked whole, often with some kind of forcemeat as a stuffing. To make serving easier, joint pheasants before consigning them to the pot; remove the skins as well if you like. Smaller birds can be partially boned if you wish, cutting down the back and carefully working round the ribs and breastbones, cutting through the wing and leg joints where they leave the body; put some forcemeat into the space and skewer or sew up the skin to return them to their former appearance. The carcasses can be used to make stock for the dish, and the birds are easier to deal with at the table.

All game birds are good with the rich wine sauces distantly derived from 18th-century braised dishes (see Pheasant with Port and Chestnuts, page 156). Since pheasants, especially, have lost a little of their glory, a wider variety of stews is worth experimenting with, such as Pheasant with Spiced Sausage and Peppers (see page 154), or try using one instead of the pigeons in Compôte of Pigeons (see page 145). Alternatively, take the meat off the bone and use instead of chicken in Chicken and Wild Mushrooms in a Potato Case (see page 112) or instead of venison in Venison and Mushroom Pie (see page 164). Partridges are also excellent in any dish with wild mushrooms.

Unless the birds are older than the current season (unlikely in these days of managed shoots) cooking times, even for gentle stewing, will not be long. Whole quail take about 25 minutes; partridge, 45 minutes to 1 hour; wild ducks and pheasants, a little longer.

Game Casserole

serves
4

400–500g (14oz–1lb 2oz) meat cut
from game birds and animals
as available

2 tablespoons duck or goose fat, beef
dripping or lard

1 medium onion, peeled and chopped

1 celery stick, chopped

1 medium carrot, trimmed, peeled
and chopped

2 garlic cloves, peeled and crushed

1 teaspoon ground coriander

a bouquet garni of 1 bay leaf, thyme,
marjoram, parsley and a few strips
of orange zest

200ml (7fl oz) red wine

10g (¼oz) dried porcini

200ml (7fl oz) boiling water

50g (2oz) bacon or pancetta, cut
into small dice

1 tablespoon balsamic vinegar
(optional)

salt and black pepper

Cut the meat as neatly as possible into 2cm (¾in) cubes. Heat the fat in a frying pan and add the onion, celery and carrot. Fry briskly, turning often, until they begin to turn slightly golden. Add the garlic, coriander and bouquet garni and pour in the wine. Simmer gently for 10–15 minutes, making sure that not too much liquid evaporates. Pour everything into a large bowl and allow to cool, then add the meat. Turn well in the mixture, cover and leave in a cold place overnight.

Next day, wash the porcini and put them in a small bowl. Pour over the boiling water and leave for at least 30 minutes to infuse.

Tip the meat into a strainer over a bowl. Keep the marinade that drips through, and the bouquet garni. Heat a flameproof casserole and fry the bacon or pancetta until it has yielded most of its fat. Remove the pieces and keep to one side. Blot any excess liquid off the meat, then fry it in the bacon fat. When the pieces are browned, remove from pan. Pour in the reserved marinade and bring to the boil, strain and return to the pan. Add the bouquet garni, the porcini and their soaking liquid, all the meat, and salt and pepper to taste, then return to a simmer.

Cover with greaseproof paper or foil and then the lid of the casserole. Cook in a low oven, 150°C (300°F, Gas mark 2), for about 1½ hours, or until the meat is cooked. Stir in the vinegar at the end, if using. Good with jacket potatoes and a dish of cabbage cooked with juniper berries.

Pigeon Pie

Pigeon pie is another dish that was once popular but now rarely makes an appearance on English tables. Early books contain numerous recipes for pigeons generally – the birds were easily accessible, kept in the dovecotes of large farms and manor houses. We have to make do with leaner, smaller wood pigeons, but they still make good pies. In old recipes, pigeons were used whole, but I prefer to use only the breast meat.

serves
4

6–8 pigeons
50g (2oz) butter
250g (9oz) button mushrooms,
   trimmed and sliced
4–6 rashers of lean back bacon
   – about 150g (5oz)
250g (9oz) chicken livers
6–8 sprigs thyme, leaves only

2 tablespoons parsley, chopped
2 sprigs rosemary, leaves only
1 tablespoon chives, chopped
50g (2oz) flour
1 quantity shortcrust pastry
   (see page 32)
beaten egg, for glazing
salt and black pepper

Put the pigeons in a pan into which they fit neatly, and cover with water. Bring them to the boil and simmer for about 30 minutes. Remove from the liquid and allow to cool a little. When you can handle them, cut the breasts off and any meat that can easily be taken from the legs. Put this on one side, return the bones to the liquid and continue to simmer to make a good game stock.

Melt the butter in a large pan and add the mushrooms. Cover and allow to cook until they have exuded quite a lot of liquid, then take the lid off the pan and continue to cook fast, stirring frequently, until most of this has evaporated.

Use the bacon to line a pie dish. Put the mushrooms on top. Examine the chicken livers to make sure the gall bladder (a small dark green sac) has been removed from them all, and cut each one into 2–3 pieces. Mix with the chopped herbs and distribute over the mushrooms. Then add the pigeon meat.

Put the pan in which the mushrooms were cooked back on the heat. Add the flour and stir well to make a roux. Cook gently to allow the flour to brown. Stir in enough reserved stock – about 500ml (18fl oz) – to make a fairly thick sauce and cook gently for a few minutes, stirring constantly. Season well, using about 1 teaspoon salt and plenty of pepper. Pour over the pigeon meat and allow to cool a little.

Roll out the pastry and cover the pie (see page 35). Crimp the edge and cut a couple of holes in the middle for the steam to escape, and decorate with pastry leaves and flowers from the trimmings, as imagination suggests. Brush with beaten egg. Bake in a hot oven, 200°C (400°F, Gas mark 6), for 20 minutes to set and glaze the pastry, then reduce the heat to 180°C (350°F, Gas mark 4) and cook for a further 45–50 minutes. The pie can be eaten hot but is best cold (not chilled).

NOTE: If you have no objection to bones in your pie, halve the raw birds and omit the step of boiling them, remembering that their bones will not be available for making stock to go in the pie. Cook the pie for about 20 minutes longer.

Compôte of Pigeon

We're more used to thinking of compôtes as sweet dishes of fruit, but originally the word related to the dish known as a daube. The two were actually the same thing, but when eaten hot, they were known as compôtes, and when eaten cold, they were daubes. The recipe, in name at least, can be traced back to one given by John Nott (1726) for 'pigeons in compost', larded pigeons braised and served over a ragoo of chicken livers, cockscombs, mushrooms and truffles. This more modest but still excellent recipe is based on one given by Agnes Marshall in *Mrs A. B. Marshall's Cookery Book* (1888).

serves
4

30g (1oz) butter
4 pigeons
a bouquet garni of thyme, parsley
    and a bay leaf
about 100g (3½oz) bacon, cut
    into matchsticks
12 small onions, peeled but left whole
2 large carrots trimmed, peeled and cut
    into dice about 1cm (½in) square

2–3 small white turnips, trimmed,
    peeled and cut into dice about
    1cm (½in) square
2 garlic cloves, peeled
about 400ml (14fl oz) game or
    beef stock
salt and black pepper

Melt the butter in a sauté pan or other deep pan that will hold the birds neatly. Add the pigeons, the bouquet garni, the bacon, onions and carrots. Fry fairly briskly, turning often until everything is golden. Add the turnips, garlic and about three-quarters of the stock, and bring to a simmer. Season with ½ teaspoon salt and a little pepper. Simmer uncovered for 45 minutes, or until the birds are cooked. Add a little more stock as that in the pan evaporates.

Remove the pigeons to a hot serving dish. Remove and discard the bouquet garni and skim any excess fat off the gravy. Taste, adjust the seasoning and bring the gravy back to the boil. Arrange the vegetables and bacon in a neat ring around the birds and pour the gravy over. Bread – either in the form of a good baguette, sliced in chunks, or ordinary bread toasted and cut into sippets (see page 29) – goes well with this.

Quail with Almond Sauce & Saffron Dumplings

This recipe was inspired by one for young chickens given by Robert May in 1685. His original required a bizarre collection of sweet and savoury, stewed and fried foods – a piece of showing off in grand baroque style, perhaps from an Italian source. Some of the ingredients suggested in my mind a dish of small birds in a lightly spiced sauce and garnished with brilliant green pistachio nuts and jewel-like pomegranate seeds. This is a recipe for those who like fiddling with elaborate dishes. Quail are small; I've suggested one per person, but you may wish to double all quantities. If garnishing with artichokes, the hearts preserved in oil are fine.

serves 4

20g (¾oz) butter
4 quail, trussed for roasting
250ml (9fl oz) strong game stock
a blade of mace
2cm (¾in) piece of cinnamon stick
pinch of saffron threads
1 dessertspoon boiling water
60g (2¼oz) fresh breadcrumbs
30g (1oz) butter
1 egg yolk
60g (2¼oz) blanched almonds

120ml (4fl oz) single cream
1–2 teaspoons sugar
salt and black pepper

to garnish (optional)

30g (1oz) blanched pistachio nuts
the seeds from ½ large pomegranate
a few green or red grapes, halved
artichoke hearts, cut into slivers
asparagus spears

Melt the butter in a flameproof casserole just large enough to hold the birds. Fry them quickly until lightly browned. Discard the fat. Add the stock, mace, cinnamon and ¼ teaspoon salt. Simmer the birds gently for 25 minutes, until just cooked.

While they cook, soak the saffron in the water for about 10 minutes. Process it and the soaking liquid with the breadcrumbs and butter, plus some of the egg yolk (you'll probably need only about half). Shape into 20 very small dumplings. Add these to the broth in which the quail are stewing about 5 minutes before the end of cooking time. Remove and discard the cinnamon and mace.

When the birds are cooked, remove them and the little dumplings to a warm serving dish. Put the almonds and cream in a blender and whizz together until the almonds are pulverised. Pour this mixture into the cooking liquid and bring to the boil. Cook gently for a few minutes – it will foam up, so keep an eye on it. Add about 1 teaspoon sugar, taste and adjust the seasoning – neither sweet not salt should predominate. Pour around the birds and garnish as elaborately as desired with pistachio nuts and pomegranate seeds plus anything else from the list.

Quail Pie

Quails stuffed with a highly seasoned forcemeat in the 18th-century manner make a delicious pie filling. It is not essential to partially bone the birds, but it makes them easier to manage on the plate. You will still need to warn your guests about the presence of small wing and leg bones.

serves
4

4 quails
20g (¾oz) flour, plus extra for dusting
30g (1oz) bacon or pancetta cut into
    small dice
30–50g (1–2oz) butter
140–150g (4½–5oz) chestnut
    mushrooms, sliced
400ml (14fl oz) game or beef stock
leaves from 2–3 sprigs thyme
a little grated nutmeg
1 quantity shortcrust pastry (see page
    32), or puff pastry (see page 34)
    if preferred
beaten egg, cream or milk, for glazing
salt and black pepper

for the forcemeat mixture
200g (7oz) veal
100g (3½oz) bacon
100g (3½oz) chestnut
    mushrooms, trimmed
about 10 sprigs parsley
about 6 sprigs thyme
12–14 basil leaves

For the forcemeat, put the veal, bacon and mushrooms into the goblet of a blender or food processor and whizz to a paste. Chop the parsley, thyme and basil finely and stir into the mixture. Cover and keep cool.

If boning the quails, open them down the backs and work a sharp knife around the ribcage, severing the wing and leg joints where they leave the body. Slide the knife around the breastbone, being careful not to cut through the skin where it attaches to this. Use the quail bones in the stockpot.

Spread the quail out, skin side down, and put about 1 tablespoon of forcemeat on each one. Pull the meat around the stuffing, re-forming the birds into nice neat little parcels. Skewer each one together down the back with a couple of cocktail sticks. Dip your hands in cold water and form the remainder of the forcemeat into walnut-sized balls. Flour these lightly.

Heat a small heavy frying pan and add the bacon or pancetta. Cook gently until the fat runs, then remove it with a slotted spoon and put into a deep pie dish. Add about 30g (1oz) of the butter to the bacon fat in the pan and let it melt. Put in the quail and brown them quickly on all sides, then remove. When they are cool enough to handle, remove the cocktail sticks and put the birds in the pie dish as well.

Fry the forcemeat balls until golden and remove to the pie dish. Add some extra butter if necessary, then the mushrooms, and fry briskly, stirring frequently, until they shrink and begin to turn golden. Dust in any remaining flour and stir in the stock to make a sauce. Add the thyme and season to taste with nutmeg, salt and pepper. Bring to the boil, then pour into the pie dish and allow the mixture to cool a little.

Dust a worksurface and rolling pin with flour and roll out the pastry to about 5mm (¼in) thick. Cover the pie dish (see page 35) and decorate as desired. Glaze with beaten egg, cream or milk.

Transfer to the oven and cook at 200°C (400°F, Gas mark 6) for 20 minutes to set the pastry, then reduce the heat to 180°C (350°F, Gas mark 4) and cook for a further 40 minutes.

Partridge with Cabbage

Partridges are usually treated with great respect in the English culinary tradition. Roasting was the favoured method for cooking, though it was admitted in cookery books that older birds needed stewing. The combination of partridges with cabbage, a classic of the French kitchen and good for using up birds past their youth, was noted by various writers in the early to mid-20th century. This is a variation on the theme.

serves 4

1 cabbage, preferably a pointed one, or January King
4 partridges
4 generous slices Parma ham
20g (¾oz) butter
1 medium onion, peeled and finely chopped
1 large garlic clove, peeled and crushed
2–3 juniper berries
200ml (7fl oz) white wine

a bouquet garni of a strip of lemon peel, a piece of celery, 1 sprig rosemary, 1 sprig thyme and a few stems of parsley, wrapped in a couple of green leaves from a leek
200ml (7fl oz) stock, preferably made with bones from game birds
30g (1oz) butter and 30g (1oz) flour, kneaded together
salt and black pepper

Discard any damaged leaves from the cabbage, then carefully detach 8–12 of the largest leaves from the outside. Keep them whole and put into a large pan. Bring a kettle of water to the boil, pour over the cabbage and boil for about 4 minutes. Pour into a colander and allow the leaves to drain well. Season each bird lightly with salt and pepper, then wrap in a slice of ham. Swaddle each bird up in two or three of the cabbage leaves.

Heat the butter in a flameproof casserole that will just hold the birds in one layer. Fry the onion gently until transparent, then add the garlic and juniper berries. Pour in the wine and bring it to the boil. Add the wrapped-up partridges, the bouquet garni, and the stock. Cover with a piece of buttered greaseproof paper, and then the lid of the casserole. Transfer to a low oven, 150°C (300°F, Gas mark 2), and cook for about 1 hour (or 1½ hours if the partridges are older birds).

Remove the birds to a warm serving plate. Put the casserole with the cooking liquid over low heat and add the butter and flour mixture in small pieces. Stir and heat gently until the sauce thickens. Taste and correct the seasoning.

Partridge with Juniper Berries

Juniper berries were apparently not much liked in 18th-century England, if Martha Bradley (1756) is to be believed; she comments on how strange the flavour of them was to palates unaccustomed to them, and recommends that they be soaked in boiling water before use – presumably to take away some of their bitterness. I've increased their impact by adding a little gin to the recipe as well. A small glass of white wine can be used instead if you prefer.

serves
4

4 partridges, trussed
    for roasting
4 rashers unsmoked bacon
20g (¾oz) butter
2 tablespoons gin
200ml (7fl oz) strong beef stock
8–10 juniper berries

a little lemon juice
10g (¼oz) butter kneaded with
    10g (¼oz) flour
lemon slices and sippets of bread,
    toasted in the oven, to garnish
    (see page 29)
salt

Cover the breasts of the birds with bacon and tie it on with thin string. Melt the butter in a flameproof casserole or small sauté pan. Brown the birds all over, then discard any fat from the pan. Warm the gin in a ladle, set light to it and pour it flaming over the birds. Add the beef stock and juniper berries, cover and simmer very gently for about 45 minutes. Turn the birds in the cooking liquid occasionally. At the end of cooking time they should be just cooked through; test the thickest part of the legs and cook a little longer if necessary.

Remove the birds from the cooking liquid and keep warm. Strain the juices into a clean pan and add a squeeze of lemon juice. Taste and add salt if necessary. Distribute the butter and flour mixture over the surface of the liquid, shaking the pan so that it is absorbed. Heat gently until it just comes to the boil and the sauce thickens slightly. Pour round the birds and serve garnished with slices of lemon and sippets.

Pheasant with Spiced Sausage & Peppers

This recipe is old-fashioned in the sense that it is based on one first published 60 years ago, by Elizabeth David in her book *French Provincial Cookery* (1960). This dish is very different to standard game recipes, and well worth trying out.

serves 4–6

2 tablespoons butter, duck or goose fat
1 pheasant, jointed into 8 pieces
about 1 tablespoon flour, for dusting
140g (4½oz) unsmoked pancetta
   or bacon, in one piece
12 small shallots, peeled
4 garlic cloves, peeled
2 tablespoons brandy
1 fresh red chilli (optional), strings
   and seeds removed, cut into fine
   slices or tiny dice

a bouquet garni of several sprigs
   oregano, thyme, parsley and a
   couple of strips of orange zest
200g (7oz) Spanish chorizo sausage,
   cut into 1cm (½in) lengths
1 red pepper, strings and seeds
   removed, cut into 1cm (½in) dice
1 yellow pepper, strings and seeds
   removed, cut into 1cm (½in) dice
200ml (7fl oz) game or chicken
   stock

Melt the butter or fat in an flameproof casserole. Pat the pheasant joints dry, then shake the flour over them. Brown them quickly in the fat and set aside.

Cut the pancetta or bacon into dice about 1cm (½in) square and add them to the fat. Cook fairly briskly, stirring from time to time, until the fat is translucent. Add the shallots and continue to cook, stirring, so that they start to brown in places. Stir in the garlic cloves and cook a moment longer.

Warm the brandy in a ladle, let it catch light and pour over the bacon mixture. Shake the dish until the flames die down, then return the pheasant to the pan. Add the chilli if using, and the bouquet garni. Put the chorizo on top, then the peppers. Pour in the stock. Cover tightly and simmer over very low heat for about 1 hour, or cook in the oven at 160°C (325°F, Gas mark 3) for 1–1½ hours.

At the end of cooking time, uncover, stir well and taste. The bacon and sausage should have given enough salt to the sauce. Serve with plain boiled rice.

Pheasant with Port & Chestnuts

A recipe that draws inspiration from the dishes *à la braise* from the 18th century. I've suggested leaving the pheasant whole, but for easier serving it can be cut into quarters before cooking.

serves 3–4

100g (3½oz) unsmoked bacon or pancetta, cut into cubes

1 pheasant, prepared as if for roasting

a little butter or oil – about 2 tablespoons

200g (7oz) shallots, peeled and finely chopped

2 garlic cloves, peeled and crushed

8 juniper berries, crushed

100ml (3½fl oz) port – tawny for preference

a bouquet garni of 1 sprig rosemary, 2–3 sprigs parsley, 2–3 sprigs thyme and 2 bay leaves

200ml (7fl oz) strong beef or game stock

200g (7oz) cooked, peeled chestnuts (use canned or in vacuum packs)

1 tablespoon arrowroot (optional)

salt and black pepper

Preheat the oven to 150°C (300°F, Gas mark 2). Heat a heavy, flameproof casserole and add the cubes of bacon or pancetta. Allow them to cook gently so that they brown slightly. When they have yielded their fat, remove them with a slotted spoon and keep on one side. Brown the pheasant in the fat, turning it so that all sides colour slightly. Remove and put it with the bacon or pancetta.

If necessary, add a little butter or oil to the casserole and add the chopped shallots and crushed garlic. Cook gently until transparent. Stir in the juniper berries, then add the port and allow it to bubble. Add the bacon and the pheasant back to the casserole, then put in the bouquet garni and the stock.

Bring to the boil, cover with foil and the lid, and place in the oven. Cook for 1 hour, then test to check that the bird is cooked: a tender young bird may be done by this point, but if you like the meat well done, it may need another 30 minutes, and an older bird takes longer. Stir in the chestnuts during the last 10 minutes of cooking; since they are pre-prepared, they only need to be heated through.

When it is done, taste the gravy and add a little salt and some pepper. For a thickened gravy, strain the cooking juices into a small pan. Skim and discard any excess fat. Mix the arrowroot with a little water and stir into the gravy. Bring to the boil to give a glossy, thickened sauce.

Carve the pheasant, if whole, and serve with the sauce poured around it. A purée of celeriac goes well with this.

Venison, Hare & Rabbit

VENISON, the meat of several deer species, is highly prized, as is hare. Both animals of the chase, they were much liked by those who could obtain their meat. Rabbit, though, had a more ambiguous status. This meant that it has been the subject for high-class dishes and also available to the rural poor – sometimes legally, sometimes poached. Some recipes for these animals have become distinctive dishes of the English kitchen.

Venison has always been treated with enormous respect in the British kitchen. Stewing was not a preferred method for cooking it, although it was admitted by 17th- and 18th-century cooks that the shoulder, highly seasoned, boned and rolled, was good braised – or, as we might think of it, as a pot roast. Venison and pastry usually implied a pasty, usually involving a quarter of the animal and elaborate decoration, as much a method of preserving the meat for a short while as anything else. The development of deer farming in the latter half of the 20th century has expanded the repertoire of English dishes involving venison.

Hare, a strongly flavoured dark meat, has also given the English kitchen a classic in the form of Jugged Hare (see page 172). This originally required the hare, liquid and seasonings to be put into a tall earthenware pot, which was left to stand in a pan of boiling water for several hours. Recipes for hare are more variable than its status as a classic might suggest, but slow cooking and high seasoning are two major attributes.

Rabbit, as a pale meat with a relatively delicate flavour, was often made into a fricassée, although it was sometimes the subject of recipes such as a florendine, an 18th-century dish in which the bodies were boned, stuffed and rolled up; the heads were skinned and left on to stare at the diners from the sauce. Rabbit pie (see Shropshire Pie, page 181) was a more bucolic (and enduring) treatment, recorded in the same century.

Cooking Rabbit, Hare & Venison

While there are obvious differences between the three meats, they are all lean and share a tendency to be dry when cooked. Stewing is a good method for any of them, especially meat from the forequarters. It keeps the meat moist, makes it tender, and is especially good for animals of uncertain age.

Most rabbit available in this country is from wild animals. They are relatively small; expect about four portions from one. They are easy to joint, and their flavour is improved by 1 hour's soaking in tepid water, or even a more elaborate brine (see page 176). When stewed slowly, they should take only 1½–2 hours to cook, maybe less. Light, herby or aniseed flavours such as thyme or tarragon go well with them, and white wine or a well-made cider are good cooking liquids.

Hares are quite large. One should feed six people easily, and may well stretch to eight, as the copious amounts of well-flavoured gravy they produce helps mop up more bland accompaniments. Unless you are confident about your skills, it is better to ask the game dealer or butcher to joint them. It is important to stew the meat slowly, using very low heat on the hob or in an oven, or use a slow cooker. Cloves and basil are good flavourings, and red wine or port is often suggested for part of the cooking liquid. Stews in the tradition of jugged hare can be made into highly spiced dishes. Hare is also good in plainer stews and with dried fruit.

Hares and rabbits arrive with the pluck – heart, liver and kidneys – still in place. If you wish to use these, add the heart to the stew at the start of cooking; it will need the long, slow treatment. Kidneys and liver are better poached towards the end of cooking time and added at the finish; cut the liver into pieces first.

Venison is more accessible than previously. Changes in the countryside have led to wild deer (especially roe) becoming more abundant than in the 19th and early 20th centuries, and deer farming has also made it easier to buy and relatively inexpensive. Like hare, it benefits from long, slow stewing, especially the meat from the shoulder joints. Wine-rich stews based on the ragoos and braises of the past are excellent methods for cooking the meat (see Venison à la Bourguignonne, page 169). Any method that is good for beef will also work with venison.

Rabbit, hare and venison stews are relatively good tempered and reheat well; a boned rolled shoulder of venison is an exception to this rule, the meat becoming dry and any gelatinous bits setting to gristle. Stews made with smaller pieces of venison don't seem to suffer from this, and the flavour improves.

Venison & Mushroom Pie

This recipe is adapted from the robust pub-lunch tradition. The pie is more usually made with beef (which works equally in this recipe), but it is a good way of using stewing venison.

serves 4

1 medium onion, peeled
60g (2¼oz) lard, beef dripping
    or light oil such as sunflower oil
2 garlic cloves, peeled
leaves from 2 sprigs rosemary
250g (9oz) button mushrooms,
    trimmed and sliced
500g (1lb 2oz) stewing venison,
    cubed

30g (1oz) flour, plus extra for dusting
150ml (5fl oz) red wine
about 300ml (10fl oz) game
    or beef stock
1 tablespoon chopped parsley
leaves from 4–5 sprigs thyme
1 quantity puff pastry (see page 34)
beaten egg, cream or milk, to glaze
salt and black pepper

Chop the onion fairly finely. Heat half the fat or oil in a large frying pan and add the onion. Let it cook quite briskly, stirring frequently. Chop the garlic and rosemary leaves small and add them to the onion. Keep frying and stirring until the onion are just beginning to go brown. Remove from the pan with a slotted spoon and put in a casserole.

Fry the mushrooms in the fat remaining in the pan. Keep the heat quite high so that any juice they exude evaporates. When they have browned a little add to the onion mixture.

Toss the venison in flour. Add the remainder of the fat to the frying pan if necessary and brown the venison in batches, transferring it to the casserole when done. Dust any remaining flour into the frying pan and stir to absorb any residual fat. Pour in the wine and keep stirring, scraping up the residues from the base of the pan. Add two-thirds of the stock and bring to the boil, stirring constantly. Add the chopped parsley, thyme, 1 teaspoon salt and some black pepper. Pour over the meat and onions in the casserole. Stir, cover tightly and transfer to a low oven, 140°C (275°F, Gas mark 1), for 2½ –3 hours. Check occasionally and stir in the remaining stock if the mixture seems dry.

At the end of this time, the meat should be tender. Skim off any excess fat, taste and correct the seasoning. Pour into a deep pie dish.

Dust a work surface with flour and roll out the pastry. Cover the dish (see page 35), decorating the pie as desired. Brush with egg wash, cream or milk.

Bake at 220°C (425°F, Gas mark 7) for 15 minutes to raise and set the pastry, then reduce the heat to 180°C (350°F, Gas mark 4) and cook for another 30 minutes, until the filling is thoroughly hot.

Meat & Potato Pie with Venison

Meat and tatie (potato) pie was a standby of my grandmother's, a frugal dish that stretched a relatively small amount of meat round a large family. Similar pies remain popular in the textile belt of south-west Yorkshire and south-east Lancashire. This is an upmarket version.

serves 4

450g (1lb) stewing venison, cut into dice
pinch of nutmeg
1 garlic clove, peeled and sliced
100g (3½oz) shallots, peeled and cut into slices
75ml (2½fl oz) good stock made from venison or beef bones
20g (¾oz) butter

1 tablespoon chopped parsley
1 teaspoon chopped rosemary
1 teaspoon chopped thyme
750g (1lb 10oz) potatoes, peeled and sliced thinly
1 quantity shortcrust pastry (see page 32)
salt and black pepper

Put the venison in the base of a deep pie dish. Season with ½ teaspoon salt, some coarsely ground black pepper and grated nutmeg. Add the garlic and shallots and pour over the stock. Cover with buttered greaseproof paper or some lightly greased foil. Put in the oven and cook at 160°C (325°F, Gas mark 3) for 1½ hours.

At the end of this time, put the butter in a large frying pan and heat it just enough to melt it. Turn off the heat and stir in the chopped herbs and ½ teaspoon salt. Stir in the sliced potatoes. Remove the meat from the oven and spread the potato mixture over the top. Replace the paper or foil cover and return to the oven on the same temperature for another 1–1½ hours.

To finish the pie, roll out the pastry. Remove the dish of meat and potatoes from the oven, turning the heat up to 200°C (400°F, Gas mark 6) as you do so. Give it a few minutes to cool a little, then cover with the pastry (see page 35). Crimp the edges and cut a hole for the steam to escape. Return to the oven for 15–20 minutes to set and brown the pastry.

Serve hot with some steamed broccoli, or shredded cabbage cooked with a little bacon and a few juniper berries.

Venison with Plums or Damsons

The idea for this recipe came partly from a friend who cooks beef with damsons, and partly from an extension of the sweet–sour flavour of redcurrant jelly, so often used with game in the English kitchen. Damsons have a very short season of 2–3 weeks. Use them if available, otherwise use plums and add a little damson jam or jelly for tartness.

serves
4

50g (2oz) butter
1 medium onion, peeled and
    finely chopped
100g (3½oz) carrot, trimmed,
    peeled and finely chopped
100g (3½oz) celery, finely chopped
1 garlic clove, finely chopped
1 generous tablespoon flour
500g (1lb 2oz) stewing venison, cut
    into pieces about 3cm (1¼in) square

100ml (3½fl oz) port
about 300ml (10fl oz) water
250g (9oz) damsons or other red
    plums, stones removed
3 tablespoons damson jam or jelly
    (if using plums other than damsons)
6 juniper berries, bruised
4 cloves
sugar, if needed
salt and black pepper

Heat half the butter in a suitable pan or flameproof casserole. Add the onion, carrot, celery and garlic. Fry briskly, turning often, until the volume is much reduced and the onion is starting to turn golden brown at the edges. Remove with a slotted spoon and put to one side.

Flour the meat. Add the remaining butter to the pan and turn the meat in it, just enough to brown it on all sides. Add the vegetables back to the pan and scatter in any remaining flour, stirring well. Pour in the port and allow it to bubble. Then stir in enough water to make a sauce. Add the damsons or plums and the damson jelly, the juniper berries, cloves, 1 scant teaspoon salt and some black pepper. Stir well, cover, and cook in a low oven, 140°C (275°F, Gas mark 1), for about 3 hours, or until the venison is tender. Taste and correct the seasoning; if damsons alone have been used, a little sugar may be needed to counteract their tart flavour.

Good bread is the best partner for this dish.

Venison à la Bourguignonne

Meaty stews of this type with red wine, mushrooms and onions, crept into English cookery after the Second World War. The recipe was originally intended for beef, but works well with venison. The sauce of red wine enriched with bacon, mushrooms and little onions recalls the rich ragoos of 18th-century, French-influenced cookery.

serves 4

500g (1lb 2oz) stewing venison, cut into slices about half the size of a postcard and 5mm (¼in) thick
1 medium onion, peeled and sliced
1 garlic clove, peeled and crushed
4 juniper berries, bruised
75ml (2½fl oz) red wine
1 tablespoon olive oil
about 40g (1½oz) butter or beef dripping
2 rashers bacon, cut into strips

8–10 tiny onions, peeled
120g (4oz) button mushrooms, trimmed and sliced
20g (¾oz) flour
175ml (6fl oz) beef stock
a bouquet garni of parsley, thyme, marjoram, a bay leaf and a strip of orange peel
salt and black pepper

Put the venison, onion, garlic, juniper berries, wine and olive oil in a bowl. Add 1 scant teaspoon salt and a generous grind of pepper. Cover and leave to marinate overnight.

The next day, tip the meat into a sieve over a bowl and allow to drain, reserving the marinade. Melt half the butter or dripping in a heavy casserole and add the bacon. Cook gently and remove when it shows signs of crisping. Add the little onions and fry, turning often, until they start to develop golden patches. Remove them and add to the bacon. Cook the mushrooms in the same fat until soft. Lift out with a slotted spoon and put aside with the bacon and onions.

Toss the drained meat (don't worry too much about disentangling the onion) with the flour. Add more butter or dripping to the pan if necessary and brown the pieces. Then pour in the marinade, stirring well. Gradually add the stock, stirring while the mixture comes to the boil.

Put the bouquet garni in among the meat, cover, and transfer to a low oven, 140–150°C (275–300°F, Gas mark 1–2), for about 3 hours. Towards the end of cooking, stir in the bacon, mushrooms and onions. Taste and correct the seasoning as necessary.

Serve with jacket potatoes, mashed potato, or papardelle tossed with a little butter and chopped parsley.

Hare with Prunes & Raisins

Sweet–sour flavours are often used with hare. In Britain, this taste seems limited to redcurrant jelly. Recipes of European origin using other ingredients are occasionally quoted in books from the 20th century. This one is based on a recipe given by Mrs Leyel and Olga Hartley in *The Gentle Art of Cookery* (1925). They suggest making this with the forequarters of the animal, to accompany a roast of the saddle and hindquarters; this would make a dish to feed six. The quantities below are enough for three.

serves 3

the forequarters of a hare
30g (1oz) butter
1 large onion, peeled and finely chopped
4 tablespoons port
500–600ml (18fl oz–1 pint) stock
    made from the bones of the hare,
    or other game, or beef

100g (3½oz) prunes, stoned
50g (2oz) raisins
salt and black pepper sugar

to garnish
3 slices white bread
50g (2oz) butter

Remove the meat from the bones of the hare and cut into neat pieces about 2cm (¾in) square. Melt the butter in a flameproof casserole and brown the meat quickly. Remove it and keep on one side while you cook the onion in the same fat until it begins to turn transparent. Add the meat back to the pan, stir in the port, about half the stock and the dried fruit. Season with some black pepper and 1 scant teaspoon salt. Simmer over the lowest possible heat for at least 2 hours. Stir from time to time and top up with stock as necessary. Alternatively, cook in a low oven, 140°C (275°F, Gas mark 1) or lower if possible, for 3–3½ hours.

Just before serving, cut the crusts off the bread and cut the slices in neat triangles or other shapes as desired – kite shapes are cited in the original recipe; hearts cut with a pastry cutter would be a nice alternative. Melt half the butter in a large frying pan and fry the croûtons over gentle heat, adding the remainder of the butter at the point when they are turned to cook the other sides. They should be golden and crisp. Drain on kitchen paper.

Pour the cooked stew into a serving dish and garnish with the croûtons.

Jugged Hare

The low oven of an Aga or a slow cooker is good for cooking this. I always let it go cold and reheat the next day, which allows the highly spiced sauce to mellow. Thickenings are best added immediately before serving. Because it is difficult to obtain hares with their blood (unless you know a really good game dealer or can get them directly from the person who shot them), this recipe uses a thickening of butter and flour.

serves
6

1 hare
1 scant teaspoon peppercorns
1 teaspoon ground cinnamon
8 cloves
1 blade mace or ½ teaspoon
    ground mace
seeds from 4 cardamom pods
pinch of cayenne
50g (2oz) butter
2 rashers bacon, about 60g (2¼oz),
    rinds cut off and cut into small dice
300ml (10fl oz) red wine
600ml (1 pint) well-flavoured game
    or beef stock
a bouquet garni of a bay leaf, 2 sprigs
    thyme, 2 of marjoram, a few sprigs
    parsley, and 2–3 sprigs basil

juice of ½ lemon
1 generous teaspoon redcurrant
    jelly or 1 teaspoon sugar
30g (1oz) flour kneaded with
    30g (1oz) butter
salt

for the forcemeat balls
1 quantity forcemeat (see page 26)
pinch cayenne or hot chilli powder
the liver of the hare, cooked in boiling
    water for 3 minutes (optional)
2 small shallots, peeled and finely
    chopped (optional)
30g (1oz) butter, for frying

Take the meat off the hare, cutting it into pieces about the size of an egg. Grind the whole spices and mix together with the cayenne and 1 teaspoon salt. Rub the mixture over the pieces of hare and allow them to marinate for about 30 minutes.

Melt the butter in a frying pan and add the bacon. Let it cook gently until the fat runs, then put in the spiced hare. Brown it quickly on all sides. Pour in the wine and let it bubble, then add the stock and bring the mixture to a simmer. Add the bouquet garni. Transfer the mixture to a casserole and cook in a low oven – 140°C (275°F, Gas mark 1) or lower if possible – for 4 hours, or use a slow cooker according to the manufacturer's instructions.

At the end of the cooking time, check that the meat is tender. Taste, then stir in lemon juice, redcurrant jelly or sugar and any extra salt you feel is required. Dot the flour and butter mixture over the surface of the sauce and shake to incorporate it into the mixture. Heat gently until lightly thickened.

Make up the forcemeat as directed on page 26, incorporating the cayenne or chilli, plus the liver of the hare and the shallots if desired. Fry the forcemeat balls gently in butter, turning frequently, for about 10 minutes. Serve the jugged hare piled on a platter with some of the sauce and the forcemeat balls around it. Hand the rest of the sauce separately.

Good bread or plain mashed potatoes are both possible accompaniments; Norfolk dumplings, made from bread dough cooked by boiling are another possibility (see page 25). Polenta, either freshly cooked or reheated (see page 175), is an excellent, if not very English, partner for this dish.

Hare & Beer Stew

Beer, sometimes suggested for basting roast hare, has been used as the cooking liquid for this simple stew, which is less complex in flavour than jugged hare but still deeply meaty. A winter ale, or a brown ale with a slightly sweet, nutty character and not too much bitterness, is best.

serves
6

1 hare
90g (3¼oz) fat bacon, rinds removed
1 large onion, peeled and finely
    chopped
150g (5oz) carrot, trimmed, peeled
    and cut into small dice
150g (5oz) turnip, trimmed, peeled
    and cut into small dice
250g (9oz) celeriac, trimmed, peeled
    and cut into small dice
3 garlic cloves, peeled and crushed

45g (1¾oz) fat for frying – butter, lard,
    goose or duck fat, dripping
60g (2¼oz) flour
300ml (10fl oz) beer, preferably one
    with a rich, sweetish flavour
300ml (10fl oz) strong beef stock
a bouquet garni of 1 bay leaf and a
    couple of sprigs each of rosemary,
    thyme, basil and parsley
salt and black pepper

The hare can be used either in joints or cut off the bone, as preferred; the cooking time will be about the same. Cut the bacon into small dice and cook in a large flameproof casserole or a frying pan until it begins to brown lightly and has given up its fat. Remove the bacon pieces and keep on one side.

Add the onion, carrot, turnip, celeriac and garlic to the fat in the pan. Cook briskly, turning often, until the pieces begin to brown slightly at the edges. Remove them and add to the bacon.

Add the extra fat to the pan. Dust the pieces of hare with flour and brown them quickly, then put them with the bacon and vegetables. Add any remaining flour to the fat in the pan and stir it into the fat. Pour in the beer, stirring well and allow it to come to the boil. Stir in about half the beef stock. Add the bouquet garni, 1 teaspoon salt and a generous grind of black pepper. Return the bacon, vegetables and hare to the mixture and bring to a gentle simmer. Transfer the contents of the pan to a casserole. Cover with foil or greaseproof paper, then the lid of the casserole.

Cook in a low oven, 140°C (275°F, Gas mark 1) or lower if possible, for 3–3½ hours, or until the pieces of hare are tender. Add the remainder of the stock if the stew is drying out. Skim any excess fat before serving. Best chilled and reheated the next day.

Polenta

Although it has no basis at all in English tradition, one of the best accompaniments for a hare stew is polenta. Make it up according to the directions on the pack some time before needed and pour it into a lightly buttered baking dish, making a layer between 1cm (½in) and 2cm (¾in) thick.

Leave to cool, then cut it into squares or triangles. Put these in a buttered baking dish, overlapping as if making bread and butter pudding. Drizzle over a little melted butter and add a dust of grated Parmesan. Bake in the oven at 180°C (350°F, Gas mark 4) for about 20 minutes.

Rabbit with Tarragon & White Wine

The mildly aniseed flavour of tarragon was not traditionally used with rabbit in British cookery, but comes from French- and Italian-influenced recipes. It provides an excellent alternative to the more usual English 'sweet herbs' such as thyme.

serves
4

1 rabbit, jointed

for the brine
50g (2oz) coarse salt
1 litre (1¾ pints) cold water
12 juniper berries, crushed
12 peppercorns, bruised
2 teaspoons fennel seeds
1 garlic clove, peeled and sliced

for cooking the rabbit
30g (1oz) butter
2 celery sticks, washed and
    finely chopped
2 garlic cloves, peeled and crushed
250ml (9fl oz) white wine
about 100–150ml (3½–5fl oz)
    stock – chicken, rabbit or game
1 tablespoon chopped tarragon,
    plus extra leaves to garnish
salt and black pepper

For the brine, put the salt in a pan and add about one-third of the water. Heat, stirring constantly, until the salt has dissolved. Remove from the heat, pour into a large bowl and add the rest of the water and the other ingredients. When the brine is completely cool, put the rabbit joints in, cover, and leave in a cold place for a few hours or overnight.

To make the stew, melt the butter in a frying pan and add the celery. Cook gently for 5–10 minutes, but don't let it brown. Stir in the garlic, cook for a moment longer, then remove the celery and garlic to a casserole.

Take the rabbit joints out of the brine and dry with kitchen paper. Brown the meat in the butter, then add the joints to the casserole. Add the white wine to the frying pan and allow to bubble for a couple of minutes, scraping the base of the pan with a wooden spoon to scrape up any residues left from frying. Pour over the meat and add about two-thirds of the stock and all the tarragon. Season with about ½ teaspoon salt and some pepper.

Cover and simmer very gently, or cook in a moderate oven, 180°C (350°F, Gas mark 4), for 1 hour, or until the rabbit meat is tender. Add more stock if it seems to be drying up.

Remove any excess fat from the surface of the stew, taste and correct the seasoning. Garnish with a little fresh tarragon and serve with mashed potato.

Rabbit with Cider & Dumplings

serves 4

1 rabbit, jointed
brine (see page 176), optional

for the marinade
400ml (14fl oz) cider
zest of 1 lemon, finely grated
2 garlic cloves, chopped
8 juniper berries, bruised
a bouquet garni of several
    sprigs parsley and thyme
    and 2 sprigs rosemary

for the stew
100g (3½oz) bacon, cut into lardons
about 30g (1oz) butter
1 medium onion, finely chopped
about 30g (1oz) flour
salt and black pepper

for the dumplings
1 quantity dumpling mixture
    (see page 24)
1 tablespoon chopped parsley
leaves from 2–3 sprigs thyme, chopped

Put the rabbit in a bowl and pour over the brine, if using. Leave in a cool place for a few hours, then drain, discarding the brine. Rinse the bowl and replace the pieces of rabbit. Mix the marinade ingredients, pepper thoroughly and pour over the rabbit joints. Cover and leave overnight.

When ready to cook the stew, drain the rabbit and reserve the marinade. Add the bacon to large frying pan and let it cook gently until all the fat has run out. Remove the bacon to a dish. Add the butter and fry the onion fairly briskly until it is translucent. Remove with a slotted spoon, allowing as much fat as possible to run back into the pan or casserole. Put the onion with the bacon.

Pat the rabbit joints dry, dredge them with the flour and fry them in the remaining fat until lightly browned. Dust in any remaining flour and pour in the marinade. Add the bacon and onions, stirring well, plus ½ teaspoon salt and a generous amount of black pepper. Transfer the pan contents to a casserole. Cover, put in the oven and cook at 140°C (275°F, Gas mark 1), for 1½ hours.

Make up the dumpling mixture, incorporating the herbs, and use a spoon to drop pieces the size of a large walnut on to the top of the stew. Return to the oven for a further 20 minutes. Finally, turn the oven up to 180°C (350°F, Gas mark 4) and cook for another 10 minutes to help the dumplings cook through.

Shropshire Pie

There was a strong association between this recipe for rabbit and pork pie and the county of Shropshire. The one given here is based on one given by Richard Bradley in *The Country Housewife and Lady's Director* (1732). Belly pork, skinned and boned, is a good cut to use.

serves 4

1 rabbit
brine (see page 176), optional
400g (14oz) fat pork
pinch of nutmeg
40g (1½oz) bacon
40g (1½oz) breadcrumbs
½ teaspoon lemon zest
a few sprigs thyme or marjoram

1 tablespoon chopped parsley
15g (½oz) butter
75ml (2½fl oz) red wine
75ml (2½fl oz) stock
1 quantity puff pastry (see page 34)
beaten egg, cream or milk, to glaze
salt and black pepper

Brine the rabbit as directed on page 176. Drain and cut as much meat as possible off the bones. Cut into neat pieces and reserve; remove the liver and kidneys and keep on one side (the remainder is best made into stock, a little of which can be used in the pie).

To assemble the pie, cut the pork into pieces about 2cm (¾in) square and mix with the rabbit meat. Put this in the bottom of a deep pie dish. Season with a scant ½ teaspoon salt, a generous amount of pepper and grated nutmeg.

Put the liver and kidneys of the rabbit together with the bacon, breadcrumbs, lemon zest, the leaves from the thyme or marjoram, and a little pepper in a food processor or blender and whizz to a paste. Stir in the parsley. Shape this mixture into walnut-sized balls and distribute over the pork and rabbit meat. Cut the butter into small cubes and dot over the mixture. Pour in the red wine and the stock.

Roll the pastry quite thinly and cover the pie. Brush over with egg, cream or milk. Set to bake in a hot oven, 220°C (425°F, Gas mark 7), for 15–20 minutes to raise and set the pastry, then reduce to 180°C (350°F, Gas mark 4) and continue to bake for 1¼ hours. Keep an eye on it and reduce the heat slightly if the pastry shows signs of browning too quickly.

Fish

ENGLISH COOKERY seemed to forget the idea of stewing fish sometime in the 19th century. Poaching, yes; stewing, not really. Were the two ideas the same? Previous generations blithely plunged all sorts of fish into hot water, with or without added seasonings, and called the results a stew. Perhaps the change was more apparent than real, and linked to the usage of words. Recipes from the 17th century indicate that stewing often meant simple, fast cooking in water. The idea of the court-bouillon – a mixture of water, wine and herbs – made its way into English cookery from French, probably in the mid- to late 17th century. This was swiftly followed by increasing elaboration, as fish stews followed the trend in the 18th century towards complicated dishes with luxurious ragoos and garnishes. The habit of adding meaty stocks to these seems especially strange to us. A trend back to simplicity returned in the 19th century and lasted until after the Second World War.

Our ancestors who lived near the coast, or perhaps on an inland port on an estuary, enjoyed an extraordinary variety of locally available fish – including soles, turbot and lobster. Salmon was commonplace, caught from wild populations migrating up rivers to spawn. Oysters, cheap and plentiful, were routinely added to savoury dishes of all kinds; mussels took a distant second place to these.

Another major difference lay in the variety of fish that cooks were expected to handle. Eels, carp, perch, pike, tench, trout and crayfish all appear to have been common; sturgeon and lampreys were not unknown. The range of freshwater fish, in particular, is startling to us. Rivers were relatively unpolluted; the ornamental lakes of landscaped gardens, such as those of Fountains Abbey and Studley Royal, were stocked for recreational fishing; and artificial fishponds provided fresh fish far from the sea. Some people still observed the Catholic habit of abstaining from meat on Fridays and during Lent.

Our range has shrunk. True, many freshwater fish have to be very fresh to taste good, and can be prone to muddy flavours, or an excess of little bones, but our kitchens are poorer without them. Fish routinely available in the past are impossible to buy. Eels, whose fatty flesh made them useful for larding other, leaner fish are difficult to obtain, while oysters, once ubiquitous, are now expensive and therefore less often used.

Dishes such as a fish pie composed of layers of lobster flesh, breadcrumbs and oysters, finished with a mixture of gravy and cream – a recipe given by Dr A. Hunter in 1807 – sound utterly delicious but remain in the world of fantasy. Maybe they always were.

Cooking Fish Stews & Pies

Because of the fragile nature of fish, stews made with them run counter to the general rules of long cooking. Depending on the size of the fish, they will take 10–20 minutes to cook on even the gentlest simmer. Don't try to keep them warm for any length of time and avoid reheating, which will make the fish dry. Nor do fish stews begin with the basic operation of frying, in the way that meat ones do. White fish are generally best for stews; stocks are now overfished, so it is best to take advice on individual species – the National Trust follows Marine Stewardship Council advice (see www.mac.org). Both salmon and trout are readily available from fish farms.

Plain water can be used for stewing fish or for fish stocks and broths, as it was in the past; it was the standard liquid for Water Souchy (see page 196). Replacing part of it with an ingredient such as white wine, lemon juice, verjuice or even cider often gives a better flavour, unless the fish is straight out of a lake. 20–30 minutes is long enough to make a simple fish stock for the recipes given here. Good herbs for flavouring and garnishing fish stews include parsley, chives, lemon thyme, chervil, fennel, dill and tarragon.

Stewed fish dishes in the past were often thickened with flour and butter added at the last minute, or with a roux. Using potato to give body to a fish stew never seems to have made its way into upper-class English cookery, nor does adding cream to enrich a simple stock. Both occur in the British-influenced cookery of New England; this may have derived from the food of other countries, or of the rural poor in Britain, whose traditions have been so inadequately recorded. Both are excellent additions. Potatoes may hold their shape or dissolve partially or completely into the liquid, giving a pleasing texture.

Adding shellfish such as oysters to a fish about 5 minutes before the end of cooking time – just enough to cook them through but not to toughen them – would have won our ancestors' approval. Diced ham or lean bacon is also good with fish – try cooking some lightly at the start and adding it to the cooking liquid, or crisping small pieces of bacon to garnish fish stews.

Haddock, Leek &
Potato Stew with Mussels

This dish is recorded on the east side of the Atlantic, where lobscouse (traditional to the north-western coast of England and ports in Germany and Scandinavia) was sometimes made with salt fish. Chowder, as made on the New England coast of the USA, is a related dish. Onions were the usual vegetable, but leeks give a good flavour and pretty contrast of colour. Ask the fishmonger to skin the fish, but get him to put the skin in the parcel, together with some fish bones if possible.

500–600g (1lb 2oz–1lb 5oz) haddock, skins and bones removed and reserved
a few stalks or leaves of parsley
1 celery stalk
2 leeks, washed, trimmed and cut into 2cm (¾in) slices (keep the trimmings)

about 600ml (1 pint) water
300g (11oz) mussels
2 large potatoes, peeled and cut into 1cm (½in) dice
60ml (2fl oz) single cream
a little fresh tarragon, chopped (optional)
salt and black pepper

Simmer the fish skin, bones, parsley, celery and trimmings of leek in a pan with the water gently for 20 minutes, then strain, reserving the liquid as stock.

Pull the beards off the mussels, discarding any that don't close when tapped. Put them in a pan with a tight-fitting lid and steam over fairly high heat for a few minutes. Strain the liquor into the fish stock, and keep the mussels on one side.

Put the potatoes and sliced leeks into a pan or a flameproof casserole. Pour over the stock and season with 1 scant teaspoon salt and a little pepper. Cook for about 10 minutes, until the potatoes are just tender. Cut the haddock into slices about 2cm (¾in) thick, and put them on the top of the vegetables. Simmer for another 5 minutes, or until the fish is just done. Add the mussels and allow them to heat through.

Put the vegetables and fish into soup bowls and pour the cooking liquid over. Add a spoonful of cream to each portion and scatter with chopped tarragon.

Cullen Skink

This is a version of a traditional Scottish soup of smoked fish and potatoes. I've altered it very slightly to push it closer to North American chowder-type dishes, and give something in between a soup and a stew. It makes a good light lunch or supper.

serves
4

400–500g (14oz–1lb 2oz)
   smoked haddock
1 small onion, peeled and sliced
a bay leaf
a few peppercorns

700g (1lb 8oz) floury potatoes, peeled
   and cut into 1cm (½in) cubes
100ml (3½fl oz) single cream
salt
chopped chives or 2 spring onions,
   very finely sliced, to garnish

Put the smoked haddock, sliced onion, bay leaf and peppercorns into a pan and cover with water. Heat and allow to simmer for about 10 minutes or until the fish is cooked. Remove it from the pan (keep the cooking liquid). When the fish has cooled enough to handle, remove all the skin and bones. Flake the flesh and set on one side. Return the bones and skin to the pan, cover and simmer for about 30 minutes longer to make a stock. Strain and measure it; 600–700ml (1–1¼ pints) will be needed. If there isn't enough, make up the quantity with water.

Put the stock and the potatoes into a clean pan and bring to the boil. Let them simmer until the potatoes are well cooked and just starting to break up a little, giving body to the liquid. Stir in the fish and heat through. Taste and add more salt if desired; remember, the smoked fish may be quite salty. Stir in the cream.

Divide between four soup bowls and scatter each portion with chopped chives or a little spring onion. Serve with wholemeal bread.

Fish Pie

A fish pie of the type common in British cookery during the 20th century, with mashed potato on top; a comforting dish when well made. This version uses a sauce recipe derived from French cookery, which is particularly good.

serves
4

800–900g (1lb 12oz–2lb) floury potatoes, peeled and cut into chunks

30g (1oz) butter

50ml (2fl oz) milk

50–60g (2–2¼oz) coarsely grated cheese – Gruyère for a mild flavour, or strong Cheddar for something more English

600g (1lb 5oz) cod or haddock fillet

250g (9oz) shell-on prawns

for making stock
the skin and any bones from the fish
the shells from the prawns
150ml (5fl oz) white wine

2 celery sticks, washed and cut into 1cm (½in) lengths

about 6cm (2½in) of the green leaves from a leek, washed and cut into thick slices

a few sprigs parsley

a small carrot, scrubbed and cut into quarters

750ml (1¼ pints) water

for the sauce
30g (1oz) butter
30g (1oz) flour
75g (3oz) créme fraîche
salt and black pepper

Put all the ingredients for the stock into a pan, bring to the boil and simmer for 25–30 minutes. Strain, discarding the debris.

To make the sauce, melt the butter in a clean pan, stir in the flour and allow to cook for a moment without browning. Stir in about 300ml (10fl oz) of the fish stock to make a smooth sauce. Allow to cook gently for 5–10 minutes, adding a little more stock if it seems on the thick side (the remainder of the stock can be frozen if you have no immediate use for it). Add the créme fraîche and season with salt and pepper to taste.

In the meantime, boil the potatoes until tender, drain and mash with the butter, milk and cheese. Season with salt and pepper to taste.

Cut the fish fillets into neat slices about 2cm (¾in) wide and arrange them in the bottom of a deep ovenproof dish. Scatter the peeled prawns over the top. Pour in the sauce and top with the mashed potato. Use a fork to roughen the surface.

Bake at 190°C (375°F, Gas mark 5) for 30–40 minutes.

Trout Pie

The 18th-century recipe given by Martha Bradley (1756), which inspired this idea, required 6 trout, each weighing about 900g (2lb). It must have been quite a pie. It also demanded eels and freshwater crayfish, both now very difficult to obtain unless you know a keen fisherman or are on good terms with fishmongers who supply restaurants. I've pushed the recipe away from the rich, savoury 18th-century style towards the current taste for south-east Asian flavours, adapting to changing tastes and available ingredients just as people did in the past.

serves 4–6

6 trout, each weighing approximately 300g (11oz)
½ teaspoon salt
1 tablespoon each of chopped fresh coriander, basil, chives
300ml (10fl oz) strong fish stock
1 tablespoon fresh root ginger matchsticks
2 kaffir lime leaves
2cm (¾in) lemongrass, thinly sliced

1 hot red chilli, seeds removed, thinly sliced
150–200g (5–7oz) uncooked king prawns, peeled

for the pie crust
a little butter, for greasing
flour, for dusting
1 quantity puff pastry (see page 34)
beaten egg, cream or milk, for glazing

Have the fishmonger remove the heads and tails of the trout and fillet them. Trim off any fins and wipe the fish well. Reserve the four largest ones.

Skin the other two and blend them with the salt in a food processor to make a paste. Stir in the chopped herbs. Divide this mixture between the four whole fish, folding them over to enclose the stuffing.

To make the pie crust, take a deep pie dish and butter it well. Lay the stuffed trout in it. Dust the work surface with flour and roll the pastry out to about 5mm (¼in) thick, then cover the dish (see page 35). Brush the pastry with beaten egg, cream or milk. Bake in a hot oven, 220°C (425°F, Gas mark 7) for 15 minutes to rise and set the pastry, then reduce the heat to 180°C (350°F, Gas mark 4) and cook for another 15 minutes. Remove from the oven.

Heat the fish stock in a pan with the ginger, lime leaves, lemongrass and chilli. When it comes to the boil add the prawns. Simmer for 3–4 minutes until the prawns are cooked through – stir occasionally so that they cook evenly.

Cut through the edge of the pastry and lift it off. Pour the prawn mixture on top of the trout. Cut the pastry into neat wedges and use to garnish the pie. Serve hot with a green vegetable accompaniment.

Water Souchy

Water souchy is the anglicised name for *waterzooi*, a dish of Flemish cookery. It made several appearances in 18th-century English cookery books as a method for freshwater fish, usually perch, simply boiled in water with a bunch of parsley. 'This seems a very insipid Dish in the Description, but there is something very pretty in the Taste of the small Fish this way,' wrote Martha Bradley in 1756. She used flounders. Like her, I use sea fish, and she is right about the fish needing to be relatively small. Later versions add wine and make a fish stock for the dish, an idea I have followed here.

1kg (2lb 4oz) of white fish, mixed according to what the fishmonger has available – try haddock or cod, sea bass and lemon sole
1 small onion, peeled and sliced
1 small carrot, trimmed, peeled and chopped
1 celery stick, chopped
250ml (9fl oz) white wine

a small bunch of parsley
salt and black pepper

to serve
50g (2oz) butter, melted and mixed with 1 tablespoon chopped parsley
triangular croûtons of bread fried in butter

Remove any skin or bones from the fish, putting them in a stockpot and cutting the flesh into neat serving pieces. Keep this cool. Add the onion, carrot and celery to the fish skin and bone and cover with water. Bring to the boil and cook quickly for about 20 minutes to make a stock. Strain, discarding the debris.

Take a pan in which the fish pieces will fit in a single layer. Pour in the wine, bring to the boil and cook for a few minutes. Add the bunch of parsley and the pieces of fish and pour over the stock. It should just cover the fish – if it doesn't, add a little water. Season with 1 scant teaspoon salt and a little black pepper and bring to the boil. Simmer until the fish is just cooked; this will take about 7–10 minutes, depending on the thickness of the pieces.

Remove from the heat and divide the fish between soup bowls. Pour some of the cooking liquor over each portion. Put the parsley butter in a small bowl and serve this and the croûtons separately.

To Stew Soles

This recipe is based on one that appears in an early Scottish cookery book by Elizabeth Cleland: *A New and Easy Method of Cookery* (1755). A simple method for cooking soles or any other flat fish, it needs a wide shallow pan in which they will fit in one layer. Ask the fishmonger to remove the skins from the soles.

serves
2

2 small soles, each weighing about
    250g (9oz)
120ml (4fl oz) white wine
a few peppercorns
1 blade of mace
a strip of lemon zest about
    3cm (1¼in) long
100g (3½oz) shelled prawns (optional)
1 generous teaspoon butter
1 generous teaspoon flour
salt

to serve
finely chopped parsley
lemon wedges
2–3 thin slices white bread,
    for making triangular sippets
    (see page 29)

Put the soles side by side in a shallow pan and pour the wine over. Add the peppercorns, mace and lemon zest, and a good pinch of salt. Bring to a simmer, then cover (use foil if the pan doesn't have a lid) and cook over a low heat for 10 minutes. At the end of this time, the fish should be cooked through, although the upper side might not be quite done – the best way to deal with this is to put the pan under a hot grill for 2–3 minutes. Add a little water if the cooking liquid shows signs of evaporating – there should be about the same amount as at the start.

When the soles are cooked, remove them to warmed plates. Put the pan with the cooking liquid back over low heat. Remove the spices and lemon zest and add the prawns, if using. Allow them to heat through to boiling. Knead the flour and butter together and dot over the surface of the liquid, shaking the pan so that it disperses and thickens the sauce. Stir and pour over the fish.

Sprinkle with parsley, and garnish with lemon wedges and the toast sippets.

Vegetables

THE ENGLISH DIET is resolutely meaty, and vegetables play a secondary role. Sometimes they are used as a support to the main ingredient (as in the use of asparagus and artichokes as garnishes), and sometimes they appear simply as extras, in which case they were often boiled in water. Boiling, in this case, is most emphatically not stewing.

For those who were very poor, a small amount of meat, sometimes just a few pieces of bacon, added savour to pots of cabbage, dried beans or peas, or potatoes. Little of this is recorded, so we don't know to what extent these may have included dishes that had the potential to become social climbers, like the cassoulets of south-west France. The remnants of dried-pulse dishes that survived – black peas in south-west Lancashire, mushy peas – were reduced to the most basic of poverty foods, and dried pea and bean dishes from the Indian subcontinent failed to transplant when East India Company employees returned with the notion of curry in the 18th century.

Yet the British country-house tradition included huge walled kitchen gardens and some of the best gardeners in the world, skilled in growing all kinds of crops and producing out-of-season delicacies for the kitchen. From artichokes to watercress, the most delicate of spring sea kale to the largest of winter turnips, a regular sequence of vegetables was available to the landed gentry by the 18th century, and to a lesser extent to those who shopped in metropolitan markets supplied by market gardeners on the fringes of towns.

Many vegetables must have ended up in boiling water, but the 18th-century fashion for complicated food produced other dishes. Some were popular as ingredients for fricassées, notably mushrooms and various root vegetables such as parsnips (see page 213); this idea hung over into the post-war period in the form of carrots served in white sauce. Green peas *à la française* became fashionable, too, and many vegetables were put into ragoos, including onions, mushrooms and celery, cooked with strong meat stocks.

Delicacies like artichoke hearts were used in 17th-century pie fillings, as one item among many, and carrots or potatoes were cooked, mashed and mixed with sugar for sweet pie fillings. In the early 19th century, Mrs Rundell suggested a pie filling of broad beans, young carrots, turnips, mushrooms, peas, onions, lettuce, parsley, celery 'or any of them that you have' stewed in veal gravy and served under a ready-baked pie crust – very different to the Woolton Pie of mid-20th century war-time rationing (see page 214).

Cooking Vegetable Stews & Pies

Vegetables vary enormously in flavour and texture and it is difficult to formulate rules about stew-type dishes made from them. On the whole, it is better not to overcook them, but some respond well to long, slow simmering, which enhances their sweetness and allows the flavours to mellow, or helps to break down tough fibres (members of the cabbage family, however, are best cooked quickly).

Think, instead, in terms of end product. For a fricassée, cook the vegetables until just done: the result should be light and fresh, and flavours won't be improved by overcooking. Most vegetables respond well to this, the main point being to adjust cooking times – short for spring and summer asparagus or beans, longer for winter roots. The light, slightly acid sauce of a fricassée means it doesn't need meat stock to make it interesting.

In ragoos and braised dishes a strong stock, preferably a jellied beef one, is essential to the true nature of the dish. Starting the vegetables off in a little butter, followed by long slow cooking, helps to mellow the flavour and evaporate liquid, so that at the end just a little highly flavoured glaze remains to coat them. This is a particularly good method for celery (see page 212) and winter root vegetables, and small pieces of bacon make good additions.

The idea of stewing vegetables in olive oil is not traditional to English cookery, but took root sometime in the late 1950s or early 1960s, when ratatouille became popular. The idea is not specific to this dish, though – use it for onions or courgettes cooked together or alone. It is also good for combinations of summer vegetables (see Sarah's Summer Vegetable Stew, page 209), but don't overcook them.

Pulses – lentils, dried peas and beans – can be used with or without meat. Lentils and dried split peas can be cooked without soaking, but beans need to be soaked for about 12 hours and then boiled rapidly for 10 minutes. After this, drain them, add fresh water and cook gently until tender. Don't add salt until the end of the cooking time. Nearly all pulse dishes now in the British cookery repertoire have been derived from France, Spain, Italy or Asia, mostly during the last 40 years.

Peas with Cream

The idea of eating fresh green peas became fashionable sometime in the 17th century. They were often cooked with butter and herbs in the manner that we still know as *à la française*, but there were variations, such as adding cream. Serve with good bread for a light lunch or supper, or to accompany egg or cheese dishes, or plainly grilled meat or fish.

serves 4

2–4 lettuce hearts, depending on size; use Little Gem, Cos or cabbage lettuces
20g (¾oz) butter
250g (9oz) green peas (shelled weight)
2 tablespoons water
½ teaspoon salt
½ teaspoon sugar

pinch of nutmeg
1 teaspoon butter kneaded with 1 teaspoon flour (optional)
4 tablespoons double cream
a mixture of fresh chives, mint, chervil or tarragon – enough to make about 2 tablespoons when finely chopped

Remove any raggedy outer leaves from the lettuces. Cut in half lengthways, wash them and then shake as dry as possible.

Put a frying pan over very gentle heat and melt the butter in it. Add the lettuces, cut side down. Put the peas in around them. Add the water, remembering that the lettuces will produce liquid as they cook. Sprinkle in the salt and sugar and grate in a little nutmeg.

Cover the pan closely (use foil if it doesn't have a lid) and cook, very gently, for 25 minutes. Check every few minutes at the start to make sure that it isn't drying up, and towards the end to see how much juice the vegetables have yielded. If there seems to be more than a couple of tablespoonfuls, remove the cover for the last few minutes.

At the end of cooking time, remove the lettuce to a warmed serving dish (if there still seems to be a lot of juice in the pan with the peas, distribute the flour and butter mixture over the surface and heat gently, shaking the pan until the sauce thickens). Add the cream, stir well and heat until nearly boiling, then pour over the lettuce. Sprinkle with the chopped herbs and serve.

Sarah's Summer Vegetable Stew

This recipe, given to me by a friend, makes the most of late spring and summer vegetables. It is essentially an easy-going mixture of the best from the garden or the market. The onion, asparagus, broad beans and peas are essential; make up the remaining weight with a selection of the other vegetables listed. Sarah suggests crusty bread and pesto as accompaniments; I add tiny butterballs and eat it with thin slices of French bread, dried in the oven until crisp.

serves
4

200g (7oz) asparagus
100g (3½oz) broad beans
    (after podding)
100g (3½oz) peas (after podding)
500g (1lb 2oz) of other vegetables
    as available – choose from other
    bean varieties such as French,
    runner or bobby beans; mangetouts
    or sugar peas; small courgettes;
    Florentine fennel; and young,
    small globe artichokes
150ml (5fl oz) olive oil
1 large onion, chopped fairly finely
a bouquet garni of a bay leaf, thyme
    and parsley, plus summer savory
    if available
300ml (10fl oz) white wine
salt

for the butterballs
60g (2¼oz) fresh breadcrumbs
30g (1oz) butter
1 egg yolk
pinch of salt
about 1 tablespoon chopped herbs
    to taste – a fines herbs mixture
    of parsley, chives, tarragon
    and chervil is good

Make sure all the vegetables are washed and prepared as appropriate. Discard any woody bits off the end of asparagus stems and cut the rest into 2cm (¾in) lengths. Trim beans, mangetouts or sugar peas and cut into 2cm (¾in) lengths as well. Trim courgettes and cut into short lengths if very small, or dice 1–2cm (½ –¾in) square if larger.

Trim fennel, discarding any tough or blemished outer layers and cut into dice like the courgettes. Trim the stems and cut the tops off globe artichokes, then scoop out and discard the thistle-like choke from the centre. Cut them in quarters.

Heat the oil in a large flameproof casserole. Add the onion, bouquet garni and the summer savory if available. Cook over a very low heat until the onions start to turn transparent. Then add the asparagus, broad beans, peas and whatever other vegetables have been chosen. Heat through, turning them all well in the oil. Add the white wine and 1 generous teaspoon salt. Bring to a simmer and cook gently, turning occasionally, until all the vegetables are cooked through but not too soft. Taste and check the seasoning.

Make the butterballs by whizzing the breadcrumbs, butter, egg yolk and salt in a blender. Stir in the chopped herbs and form into about 20 little balls the size of hazelnuts. Drop them into the cooked vegetable mixture and continue to simmer for 5 minutes.

Serve in deep bowls, adding pesto if you wish, and hand bread or toast separately.

Stovies

A simple but extremely good method for gently stewing potatoes, traditional to Scottish cookery. Use maincrop potatoes, preferably floury varieties. The key is very gentle, slow cooking. They can be served as an accompaniment to roasts, grills, meaty stews or eaten alone as a supper dish.

serves
4

1kg (2lb 4oz) potatoes, medium in size
    and fairly even in shape
60g (2¼oz) butter
about 3 tablespoons of water
chopped parsley or chives, to garnish
salt

Peel the potatoes and cut them into slices about just under 1cm (½ in) thick. Melt the butter in a heavy-based pan or flameproof casserole. Add the potatoes and turn them well in the melted butter. Cover and turn the heat to the lowest possible. Cook for 10 minutes. Then add about ½ teaspoon salt and some water – 3 tablespoons should be enough.

Cover with the lid again and leave on very low heat to cook. Check occasionally and shake the pan or turn the potatoes gently from time to time. If they show signs of drying up, add a little more water. They will need about 50 minutes gentle cooking, by which time the slices should all be tender and some will be starting to fall apart.

Add chopped herbs as desired just before serving – not traditional, but a nice touch.

Braised Celery

A vegetable dish that has been in the English cookery repertoire for at least 200 years. It is a good side dish for roasts of game, especially venison, or as a separate vegetable course with some crusty bread, in which case omit the croûtons.

serves
4

2 large heads celery
15g (½oz) butter
1 small–medium onion, peeled and finely chopped
1 small carrot, trimmed peeled and finely chopped
1 small slice of turnip, peeled and finely chopped
a bouquet garni of a bay leaf, some thyme and parsley
about 500ml (18fl oz) strong beef stock
croûtons fried in butter, to garnish
salt

Trim the heads of celery, removing any particularly stringy outer stems. Cut in half lengthways, wash well and blanch in boiling water. Cut in half crossways as well if the stems are very long.

Melt the butter in a pan that will hold the celery neatly in one layer. Add the onion, carrot and turnip, and cover. Allow them to sweat gently for about 15 minutes, then put in the celery, cut side down. Add the bouquet garni and pour over about two-thirds of the stock. Bring to a simmer and cook gently but steadily for about 2 hours. Add more stock as it evaporates, but towards the end of cooking allow it to reduce so that it becomes a fairly concentrated glaze.

Remove the celery and put it on a warmed serving dish. Taste the cooking liquid and add seasoning if required. Strain it over the celery and garnish generously with the croûtons.

Fricasséed Parsnips

Eighteenth-century cookery writers seemed to make everything into fricassées, including most vegetables. It is a good way of dealing with parsnips, whose texture and natural sweetness respond well to this, as in a recipe based on one given by Hannah Glasse in 1747. Eat as a separate vegetable dish with good bread or use as an accompaniment to plain grilled or roast beef or pork.

serves
4

600–700g (1lb 5oz–1lb 8oz)
 parsnips, peeled
100ml (3½fl oz) white wine
120ml (4fl oz) cream beaten
 with 2 egg yolks

15g (½oz) butter kneaded with
 15g (½oz) flour
salt
pinch of nutmeg

Cut the parsnips into pieces about 4cm (1½in) long, then cut these into wedges lengthways. Cook in boiling water until tender (about 10–15 minutes), then drain.

Clean the pan and add the wine. Bring it to the boil and add the parsnips. Cook gently for a moment, then remove the pan from the heat and pour in the cream-and-egg mixture. Heat very gently but don't allow it to boil. Dot the flour and butter over the top and continue to heat gently, shaking the pan until the mixture is absorbed into the sauce, which should thicken lightly. Season to taste with salt and a little nutmeg.

Root Vegetable Pie

The original of this recipe was Woolton Pie, which became infamous during the Second World War. It was a dish of root vegetables, such as swede and parsnip, cooked under an oatmeal pie crust – plain as plain could be and apparently much disliked by a nation desperate for meat and other luxuries. I thought it would be interesting to update it with more unusual vegetables.

serves
4

300g (11oz) Jerusalem artichokes
300g (11oz) celeriac
300g (11oz) leek (white part only)
300g (11oz) waxy potatoes (such as Anya, Pink Fir Apple)
120g (4oz) well-flavoured cheese – a good Cheddar, or try Blue Stilton, cut into thin slices or crumbled

40g (1½oz) butter
40g (1½oz) flour, plus a little extra for rolling the pastry
600ml (1 pint) milk
pinch of nutmeg
1 quantity puff pastry (see page 34)
beaten egg, cream or milk, to glaze
salt and black pepper

Wash the Jerusalem artichokes, put them in a pan, cover with water and simmer for 10–15 minutes, or until just tender. Drain and cover with cold water; once they are cool enough to handle, peel off the papery skin. Cut the flesh into julienne strips. Wash and peel the celeriac and cut into julienne strips. Wash the leek and slice into thin rings. Wash the potatoes, peel them if desired and cut into julienne strips.

Put the artichokes into a deep dish, scatter over about a quarter of the cheese, and repeat with the other vegetables and remainder of the cheese.

Melt the butter in a pan, stir in the flour, then add the milk to make a sauce. Season with salt, pepper and a scrape of nutmeg. Pour this over the vegetables in the dish.

Use the extra flour to dust a worksurface and roll out the pastry. Use it to cover the dish (see page 35), trimming nicely, and making decorative leaves as desired. Make a hole for steam to escape and brush with egg, cream or milk. Transfer to a hot oven, 220°C (425°F, Gas mark 7) for 20 minutes, then turn the heat down to 180°C (350°F, Gas mark 4) and cook for a further 40 minutes.

Chestnut & Shallot Pie

This recipe began as an attempt to make a vegetarian equivalent of my grandmother's meat and potato pie, a plain but comforting dish of the farmhouse and urban industrial communities in Yorkshire and Lancashire. Along the way, it developed into something much richer. If you are not concerned with being strictly vegetarian, add about 50g (2oz) pancetta cubes, well fried and drained of their fat, to the chestnut and shallot mixture.

serves 4–6

30g (1oz) butter, plus extra for
   the potatoes
200g (7oz) shallots, peeled
8 garlic cloves, peeled
200g (7oz) cooked, peeled chestnuts
   (use vacuum packed ones)
2 tablespoons brandy
1 tablespoon chopped parsley
leaves from 1 sprig rosemary, chopped
leaves from 5–6 sprigs thyme

75ml (2½fl oz) single cream
2 tablespoons truffle paste (optional)
50ml (2fl oz) water
800g (1lb 12oz) potatoes, peeled
   and sliced
1 quantity puff pastry (see page 34)
flour, for dusting
beaten egg, cream or milk,
   for glazing
salt and black pepper

Melt the butter in a large frying pan. Add the shallots and fry gently until they begin to develop golden brown patches. Add the garlic and cook for a few moments longer. Add the chestnuts and pour in the brandy. Allow it to bubble, then stir in the herbs and cream. Add the truffle paste if using, plus the water. Taste and add salt and pepper as desired.

Put the mixture in the bottom of a deep pie dish. Layer the sliced potatoes over the top, dotting a little butter between and sprinkling lightly with salt. Dust a worksurface with flour and roll out the pastry to about 5mm (¼in) thick. Use this to cover the pie (see page 35), and decorate the top with pastry leaves if desired. Cut a hole for the steam to escape, and brush with beaten egg, cream or milk. Start the pie off in a hot oven, 220°C (425°F, Gas mark 7) for 20 minutes, then turn the heat down to 180°C (350°F, Gas mark 4) and cook for another 40 minutes or until the potatoes feel done when tested with a small knife through the steam hole. A salad of peppery or bitter leaves such as watercress or rocket is good with this.

Butterbean Casserole

The idea of eating vegetable dishes that were actually vegetarian – no bits of bacon, no meat stock – was a novel one in the Britain of the late 19th century. The Food Reform Movement did their best within the conventions of the time, trying to work out substitutes for the vast amounts of protein seen as necessary for health. At the same time, things that would now be considered good additions, such as olive oil, garlic and herbs, weren't used either because of snobbish ideas about 'greasiness' and bad breath, or simply because they weren't obtainable. The butter bean stew made by my mother probably originated with ideas from this time and I have incorporated a few things either unavailable or frowned upon in earlier days.

serves
4

150g (5oz) dried butter beans
3–4 tablespoons olive oil
1 large onion, peeled and
    finely chopped
2 garlic cloves, peeled and
    finely chopped
leaves from 1 sprig rosemary,
    finely chopped
100ml (3½fl oz) white wine
a bouquet garni of a bay leaf, a few
    sprigs parsley and some thyme
about 350ml (12fl oz) water
400ml (14fl oz) passata
    (sieved tomato pulp)
a handful of basil leaves, chopped

for the topping
4 slices good white bread, crusts
    removed, cut into triangles
about 4 tablespoons good olive oil
about 40g (1½oz) strongly flavoured
    cheese, such as Pecorino Romano
    or a good Cheddar, finely grated
1–2 tablespoons pine nuts (optional)
salt and pepper

Soak the beans overnight in cold water. Next day, bring them and the water to the boil and cook rapidly for 10 minutes. Drain, discarding the water.

Heat about 3 tablespoons olive oil in a flameproof casserole. Add the onion, garlic and rosemary. Cook briskly, stirring often, until the onion begins to brown slightly. Lower the heat and add the beans, turning them in the mixture.

Add the wine, the bouquet garni and the water. Bring to the boil, cover, and then cook either on very low heat on the hob or in a moderate oven, 150°C (300°F,

Gas mark 2) for about 1¼ hours, or until the beans are soft. Stir occasionally and check the liquid level. Add a little more water if they seem to be drying out. When they are fully softened, season with about ½ teaspoon salt and some pepper. Turn the oven up to 200°C (400°F, Gas mark 6). Add the passata in a layer on top of the beans and scatter the chopped basil over the top.

Dip the pieces of bread in olive oil (lightly, don't try to saturate them) and arrange over the top as if making bread-and-butter pudding. Sprinkle with grated cheese and scatter over the pine nuts (if using). Return the dish to the oven, uncovered, and allow the topping to brown and crisp for about 10 minutes; check from time to time to make sure that it doesn't scorch.

This is a filling dish and the best accompaniments are either a salad or some lightly cooked summer vegetables.

Further Reading

Acton, Eliza, *Modern Cookery for Private Families*, 1845 edition with an introduction by Elizabeth Ray (Southover Press, 1993)

Bradley, Martha, *The British Housewife*, 1756 edition with an introduction by Gilly Lehmann (Prospect Books, 1996)

Bradley, Richard, *The Country Housewife and Lady's Director* (1732)

Cleland, Elizabeth, *A New and Easy Method of Cookery*, 1755 edition with an introduction by Peter Brears (Prospect Books, 2005)

Cobbett, Anne, *The English Housekeeper* (1840)

Cooper, Jos, *The Art of Cookery Refin'd and Augmented* (1654)

David, Elizabeth, *French Provincial Cookery* (Michael Joseph, 1960)

Davidson, Alan, *The Oxford Companion to Food* (Oxford University Press, 1999)

Glasse, Hannah, *The Art of Cookery Made Plain and Easy*, 1747 edition (Prospect Books, 1983)

Hunter, Dr A., *Culina Famulatrix Medicinae or, Receipts in Modern Cookery* (1807)

Kenny-Herbert, Colonel A. R., *Culinary Jottings for Madras*, 1885 edition with an introduction by Leslie Forbes (Prospect Books, 1994)

Leyel, C. F. and Olga Hartley, *The Gentle Art of Cookery* (1925)

Marshall, Agnes, *Mrs A. B. Marshall's Cookery Book* (1888)

May, Robert, *The Accomplisht Cook*, 1685 edition with an introduction by Marcus Bell (Prospect Books, 1994)

Nott, John, *Cook's and Confectioner's Dictionary*, 1726 edition with an introduction by Elizabeth David (London, 1980)

Pember-Reeves, Maud, *Round About a Pound a Week*, 1910 edition with an introduction by Sally Alexander (Virago Press, 1999)

Rundell, Maria, *A New System of Domestic Cookery* (1821)

Soyer, Alexis, *The Modern Housewife* (1851)

White, Florence, *Good Things in England* (Jonathan Cape, 1932)

Index